Wow, this was a roller coaster of emotions. One page I was crying tears of happiness, and the next page tears of sadness. I was rooting for them the entire book, but each page left me with a nail biting worry. Ashley and Steven have been through so many struggles as a couple, and I love that they didn't hold back discussing these issues, as many of us have been there too and can relate. The selfless people in this book came together and created such a beautiful life and an inspiring story. Happily Evans After is the perfect name for this family because, after all the struggles and ups and downs they went through, they, in fact, got their Happily Ever After.

—KRYSTIANA, @krystianatiana

I cannot recommend this book enough!! Ashley and Steven hold nothing back in this raw and honest odyssey of their life and love. It made me feel seen in its relatability, and also inspired through the way that this couple has pushed through and overcome so many challenges. In today's world of social media-slung perfectionism and false facades, Ashley and Steven are refreshing in their authenticity. This book will remind its readers that the strength to overcome our obstacles and create the life we desire lies within each of us—and that love conquers all.

—SHANNON WILLARDSON, @shannonwillardson

If you think you know Ashley and Steven's story—just you wait!

Ashley and Steven break down the stereotype that surrounds "influencers," and share their powerful, relatable, and inspiring story. With each chapter I was on the edge of my seat, wondering what was going to happen next. Through their journey, they endured many struggles that honestly had me holding breath, waiting for that "light at the end of the tunnel." I truly feel this book can relate to so many people, no matter what season of life they are in. So be prepared to be emotional. But more than that—prepare to absolutely fall in love with this incredible couple and their story.

—MARIYAH GERBER, @mariyahgerber

In "Happily," Ashley and Steven Evans offer a raw and emotional account of their imperfect journey to parenthood. Their vulnerability and authenticity in sharing the highs and lows of not only adoption, but interracial adoption, and the impact of social media on their journey are truly commendable. To quote Ashley, "Finally, for real this time, my dream came true. I was a mom." It brought me to tears, as a fellow parent who had my own fair share of fertility experiences. Get ready to cry, laugh, and fall even more in love with this couple, their story, but most importantly, their family.

—DEMI SCHWEERS, @demischweers

Happily

FINDING JOY EVEN WHEN
LIFE IS FAR FROM A FAIRY TALE

Ashley & Steven
EVANS

Cover Design by Mackenna Cotten
Photograph by Hailey Merlo Media

Fedd Books
P.O. Box 341973
Austin, TX 78734

www.thefeddagency.com

Published in association with The Fedd Agency, Inc., a literary agency.

ISBN: 978-1-957616-37-7
eISBN: 978-1-957616-38-4

LCCN: 2023906412

Printed in the United States of America

DEDICATION

To our son, Abriel—you have brought so much joy, happiness, and love into our lives and we hope you never forget how special you are! We would relive every painful moment all over again, just to call you our son!

We love you.

TABLE OF CONTENTS

FOREWORD

"Never judge a book by its cover."

Five years ago, I got to meet my son's future parents. It's a strange process, sitting in a lawyer's office and looking at the people I would hand over a piece of my heart to in a few months, wondering if they would treat him well or if I'd ever get to see him after the moment I gave him up and he became theirs. That little lawyer's office felt huge as we ate our Jimmy John's and talked about my son's future.

When I met Ashley and Steven that day, I definitely judged them based on appearances. Who could be so perfect? Was it possible?

I wanted to see it all before I made my decision, the good, the bad, and the ugly, and before the end of this process, we definitely saw it all. The truth was, I didn't need Ashley and Steven to be perfect, I needed them to be themselves. And as we grew closer through this process, I was able to see Ashley and Steven's true heart and the love they had to give, not just to their future baby boy, but also to me. Ashley and Steven never shied away from being themselves, even as they faced the scrutiny of millions of people. I watched as they worked through financial struggles, marital problems, a newborn who won't sleep through the night, and more, while they also dealt with life in the public eye as influencers, the traveling, and all the ups and downs that came with it.

It's impossible to truly know a person from fifteen second Instagram clips or a caption under a post. I got to live this story with them, and now, you can experience it in a new and deeper way to truly understand the heart of our story and of Ashley and Steven.

I'll be grateful to Ashley and Steven forever for providing my son with a loving home and including me in this happily ever after they've sacrificed and worked to build. Our family is unconventional, but it's ours. I wouldn't have it any other way.

Makayla
Abriel's Birth Mom

INTRODUCTION

Ashley

When you have a social media platform with any kind of audience, people instantly start making assumptions about your life. It's only natural, right? And even if we try to have the most authentic platform possible, you'll never show *everything*. Whether we're putting our lives on a public forum like social media or just paying attention to what people in our local community see, it's only natural to want to show people the beautiful, fun, and meaningful part of our lives. Of course, that's not what our everyday looks like, but it's normal to want others to see and take part in the special and important moments. After all, when you've spent so long building the life you want, you want others to see the stuff you're most proud of.

While that's totally understandable, sometimes it means we put out an image that just doesn't exist. If I create a video, a photo, or a blog, I'll naturally try to put myself in the best light. I'll shoot this TikTok with the backdrop showing the right side of my room because the left side is covered in laundry. I'll write this post about a sweet thing my baby did rather than talk about the temper tantrum they just threw because I got them the "wrong" cup for their milk.

We all fight that urge to present a more perfect version of our lives—baking something tasty for new neighbors, deep-cleaning our house for guests, making sure the kids are on their best behavior at the store—all to put forward this image of perfection. And even though we know that creating these façades isn't a reflection of reality, we can't help but look at people online and wish our lives were more like theirs. Adding to the mirage is the contradictory message from lifestyle influencers who say they wish their lives could be as perfect as they portray on social media.

It's all fake. We all know it, yet we still can't help but strive for this perfect life no one is actually achieving. It makes people depressed, doubt their choices, and think that if they could only find that one perfect, ineffable thing to add to their content, they'd finally make it to this curated reality we see lifestyle influencers manifesting. Never finding that one ingredient to make their life perfect can leave a person feeling hopeless, worthless, and utterly alone. We say this because we know full well that our platform can occasionally put off the vibe that our lives are perfect or better than everyone else's. We're constantly hearing from our followers how our son must never cry or throw tantrums because we don't post his bad moods or how we must be super rich and our lives a breeze because we've found a degree of internet fame. The thing is, not only is that not our reality, it isn't anyone's reality. It's a small part of why we wanted to write this book.

INTRODUCTION

Instagram and TikTok are breezy and light platforms, so we don't like to get too intense on something you're likely just scrolling through absentmindedly or when you have a few spare minutes. Plus, there are some things about our life that we just want to keep private. Because in our real lives, we've known a lot more pain, hardship, and struggle than you'll see on our Instagram.

Despite all of that, and how much of our life is pretty ordinary, we were still able to build this life that we chronicle online. Why is that? Because for every extraordinary moment in our lives, in the midst of the ordinary moments—the stuff we all take for granted or ignore as we search for something amazing—we took the time to look around and explore every opportunity life threw at us, from the mundane to the massive. We grabbed those moments and used them to build something beautiful.

What did you see when you were a kid and thought about your future? Maybe you saw yourself as a famous movie star, gracing the silver screen in the biggest blockbusters. Maybe you saw yourself as a high-powered politician, effecting change and improving the world. Maybe your dreams were a little more personal. A spouse you loved. A family.

Sure, those dreams evolve and change as we grow and experience more of the world, but there is something almost sacred to those dreams that stick around into adulthood. They move from silly-but-nostalgic dreams like, "I always wanted to be a part-time movie star, international spy, and veterinarian when I was a kid," and become dreams that feel foundational to who we are as people as we search for what we want out of our spouse, family, and career.

And when it seems like those dreams won't be realized, or they get dashed entirely, it can feel like we're losing a part of ourselves.

If you're working to create a life centered around a particular career, losing that path can make you feel not only directionless, but also worthless. If you spent years building a life around a romantic partner and you lose them, it can be heartbreaking and make you doubt your worth, whether you're worthy of love, and if there is any hope in pressing on. When people talk about building a life they can be proud of, it's always far more than just a good job, a spouse they love, or a couple of kids. Deciding what we want our lives to look like means funneling our hopes, dreams, morals, and even parts of our souls and identities into a tangible goal. When you lose that, it's easy to feel like there isn't any point or purpose in life.

So why are you talking to a couple of social media content creators about something like this? If you've never met us, we're Steven and Ashley Evans. And we're all too familiar with that soul-deep pain of losing your core dreams and visions for your future, but we've managed to come out on the other side and build a life we love.

Chances are you've seen us goofing around on TikTok, Instagram, or YouTube in our refurbished firehouse-turned-house with our son, Abriel. And while a glance at our social media platforms might paint the picture of a perfect, "beautifully messy" life, our life is far from perfect.

Yes, our life is beautiful, but sometimes we lean *really* hard into just plain messy. But this isn't where we started as a family. In fact, this family you see before you almost didn't happen. Because before social media, before Abriel, it felt like our lives were falling apart before they even got a chance to take off.

We used the painful, wonderful, and mundane pieces to build something beautiful, and we hope more than anything that when you finish this book, you will see that you can also build a beautiful life for yourself. Life might not be going how you planned. Things might feel chaotic, scary, insurmountably challenging, or so heartbreaking that it's sometimes hard to breathe. We might not know exactly what you're going through, but we've walked through the chaos, the scary, the challenging, and the heartbreaking. You can make it through those moments too, and even if the life you always dreamed of isn't a possibility, it doesn't mean your life is over. You're just starting a new chapter. If you can take the time to stop, look around, and find the beauty in the smallest moments, you can use even the broken pieces to create a beautiful, joy-filled life. We managed to do it, and we know you can too.

If you don't believe us, grab a snack, get comfortable, and let us tell our story. Things didn't go how we thought. There were times when everything felt as far from a fairy tale as you could get, and things are far from perfect now, but we managed to find a way to our happily ever after. And if we could find ours, trust us, you can find yours, too.

1

FAR FROM A FAIRY TALE

Ashley

We'd love to tell you that our love story started in some sweeping, out-of-this-world fashion. Meeting on a train in France, spotting one another from across a glamorous party, or after some heroic, lifesaving rescue. But our story starts like so many of yours: by swiping right.

Yep, we met on a dating app in the summer of 2014. I love that about our story. I love that this exciting journey starts in a regular way. Because it drives home what I love most about this life we've built together: things can begin unremarkably, and things can go wrong, but those uneventful beginnings and wrong turns can sometimes lead us on the most epic adventures if we're just willing to take a step or two of faith.

Our early dating days did *not* include outrageous, glamorous dates or even long, lazy days hanging out together, sharing our hopes and dreams in parks and coffee shops. We didn't enjoy any of those clichés from movies or TV. Instead, from day one, we were working hard, especially when it came to Steven's property business. And by working hard, I don't just mean occasional late nights, a bit of elbow grease, and some creative budgeting to make sure ends could meet.

Steven was working to build his business from the ground up, buying properties, renovating them, and renting them out. While owning property is often misunderstood to be a no-brainer, low-effort way to make money, it was proving to be an all-consuming, exhausting business endeavor. It was a ton of work keeping up with his rental properties, renovating old homes that he bought, making repairs, and simply ensuring the properties were up to par for renters to live in.

Because of that, we spent most of our dates in his moving van turned work truck, with me precariously perched between the two front seats on a five-gallon bucket, going from a property to the hardware store, then back to work on a property. I realized that if I was interested in getting to know this man, the only way I'd get to spend real time with him was by going with him to job sites. Sure, it would have been cool if we spent the majority of our early days of dating going to extravagant places, but there was something about Steven that just pulled me in. I loved spending time with him, and whenever he talked about his business and work ethic, it was clear from the spark in his eyes that he wasn't just working to pay the bills. He was working toward something, and I realized I wanted to be a part of it. They say nothing worth having comes easily, and I saw that clearly in those early days dating Steven. We hadn't been together long, but I couldn't help but set my eyes on the future he envisioned and get excited. It was an adventure, and I was ready for whatever life had in store for us. And ultimately, it made the hard work or "unique" dates we went on seem worthwhile and a bit more fun.

My idea of a perfect date is not home repair, renovations, and supply runs at our local home improvement store, but in those days, everything was still new and exciting. Plus, neither of us thought this would be our new normal. Steven always worked incredibly hard, and it was always with the end goal of building a stable, comfortable life for his family down the road. So yeah, today might be challenging, but that hard work would pay off tomorrow. One day, we'd look back on all the blood, sweat, tears, and long hours as we sat with our successful business and beautiful home that housed our loving family, and these home improvement-filled dates would seem worth it. Right?

This was what I was holding out for. I was willing to sacrifice short-term comfort for long-term security, and we both were on the same page. A relationship, in general, is all about sacrifices, and Steven and I had that practice down early on. It can be really easy to fall into the trap of wanting that social media-perfect relationship, with lots of content that you can slap on your grid to say, "Look how cute my boyfriend is," or, "Look what my boyfriend bought me." While it can often start honestly and genuinely, it quickly can turn into making your relationship a contest with those around you and commodifying your relationship. But what Steven and I learned in those early days of our relationship is that a strong bond is built between two people willing to sacrifice and work every day to serve their partner. When the focus isn't on building a relationship that you can curate for social media but on building a life together, that's when you've got something truly life-changing.

Steven and I got into a healthy rhythm of sacrifice to make the relationship work. I was willing to do these things because I knew Steven was interested in getting to know me, and we both had similar ideas of how we wanted our future lives to look. However, I had no idea the sacrifice required on my part was about to get a lot pricier.

Not long after we started dating, Steven left for what was supposed to be a year on a mission trip to the Philippines. To be fair, the trip wasn't a surprise to me, as he'd let me know about it early on. But I assumed once the trip rolled around, we'd be on the same page about where our relationship stood. I had hoped that, at the very least, we'd be ready for the conversation. I was wrong.

I broached the conversation one day before he headed out, and I couldn't shake the pit in my stomach for some reason. I asked him the "what are we?" question the movies teach you that every guy hates. I had to know where we stood before I spent a year waiting for him. I needed to know where he saw this going, and his response was not what I expected and definitely not what I wanted.

"I don't know how much time I'm going to have to really invest in us. I don't want to force anything, but you know I don't want to lose you either."

He wanted to keep things "chill" and not label it, just see where the year takes us. I wasn't sure if I was sad or angry with his response. I guess I thought he'd either commit or get out, but this lukewarm noncommitment was the farthest thing from what I wanted. He wasn't ready for commitment. But I was. And I knew I wasn't ready to give up on us. I could have pushed it and forced him to decide, but I knew that would likely push him toward the get-out option, so I agreed.

You don't have to be a psychic to know where this is going. Shocking to no one, the non-committed commitment was insanely hard on me. Steven was far away, emotionally and physically, and the longer I waited for him, the more and more I felt like I was investing all of this time, effort, and heartache into someone who simply didn't want me the way I wanted them. I wasn't going to let myself wait an entire year for a guy who would mess around with other women while we were apart, come home, and then dump me. I deserved better than that, and I told him it was time to make a choice.

I didn't know how he'd respond, and it was often tough to get our schedules to align for a longer conversation, but I figured my feelings would be best received over email. Maybe that was just me being a bit of a chicken, but I also knew it was the only way I could be as blunt about my thoughts as I needed to be. I suspected he was seeing other girls while he was down there, which, to be fair, aligned with our "keep things chill" agreement. But I wanted him to know exactly what I was thinking and feeling and how his actions impacted me. So I was painfully honest about everything.

I told him how I felt about him but that I didn't think I could wait for him for a whole year, especially given that I knew he wasn't yet "all in." I told him how angry and sad it made me that he was seeing other girls and that I didn't want to spend all of this time pining away for a guy who wasn't thinking about me the way I thought about him. I especially didn't want to put my life on hold for a guy who could return in a year just to leave me. If he wanted to be with me, he needed to be all in. I was ready to commit to him; if he wasn't ready to commit to me, we needed to go our separate ways. Anything less was breaking my heart. I was unsure how he'd respond, but I also knew if he and I were going to have any kind of future, I would need to feel safe being open and honest, even when it was hard. I had fallen in love with Steven, and I was terrified he'd email me back and end things, but I tried to keep my spirits up, reminding myself that if it was meant to be, it would all work out somehow.

I could tell you how that went, but I'll let Steven.

Steven

When I initially left for the Philippines, I wasn't sure how I felt about Ashley. We hadn't been dating that long, and even though she was cool, it was all new. I'm a pretty logical guy, and I didn't want to lose an opportunity to do some real good in the world for a girl I had just met. But I also didn't want to blow it with a girl that could change my life. I figured since she knew about my trip from the start of our relationship, I'd just keep my plans intact, and if we were meant to stay together, it would work out.

Of course, things don't ever go as you plan. While I was thinking my biggest concern back home would be whether Ashley and I would stay together, it turned out that was only one of the storms brewing. The guy I had trusted to run my business while I was away was doing anything *but* that.

When I say I picked someone I trusted to run my business, I don't mean someone who did good work. I really trusted this person. Before I left, everyone jokingly referred to him as my son because I mentored him and looked out for him. I think it's crucial to help people, and I know from my childhood what a massive difference it can make when someone sees your potential and does whatever they can to give you opportunities.

I poured so much time, mentorship, and money into his life. I trained him in business so he could learn a trade and financially support himself. I paid for his meals and cell phone and bought him a new set of tools. I'd drive him to and from his MMA practice, and I'd never miss a chance to give him an opportunity for growth or support. I figured he'd be a no-brainer choice to run the show while I was gone, and I assumed he'd thrive with such a big opportunity. Still, I tried to make it as easy for him as possible. We arranged for him to stay in one of my unoccupied properties, kept the responsibilities on him as low key as possible, and created a relaxed work schedule that would only require him to pay a few bills, check on tenants, and keep up properties for me. He'd been working by my side for so long. I had no doubt he could do a great job.

I had no idea how wrong I would be about him.

It sucks to have someone betray you, especially when you've spent so much time fostering a relationship, building trust, and learning to care about this person. Unfortunately, this guy didn't just forget to check on some properties or miss a bill or two.

Instead, he took all of that trust, time, effort, and access I gave him and destroyed it all. In no uncertain terms, he ran my business—and by extension, my credit—into the ground. He purposefully stopped paying bills for the company and pocketed the rent money. He trashed the property I had housed him in and started ripping radiators out of other units to sell for drug money. It was a disaster. I was angry, hurt, and blindsided.

I was at a loss for what to do next. The business I had worked so hard to grow was ruined before it could take off. The person I had mentored and thought of as family proved that he didn't care about me. I was in another country, and my life back home was slowly going up in flames. And I get it. Life can be hard. I'm used to hard, and I'm used to putting in the work to achieve my goals. But this was one of the first times that something I had spent so long working toward fell apart because of the actions of someone I had trusted. I found myself back at square one, and even though it was gutting and unfair, I had to start rebuilding my life and my future, brick by brick.

As I tried to sort all that out, I received Ashley's email and realized I had some big decisions to make. The longer I stayed in the Philippines, the more things at home were destroyed. Maybe it was time for me to go home. Still, I was helping people who needed it, and I didn't want to just bail on them when my life got a bit uneasy. So I called one of my best friends from home for advice.

It felt like my entire life was blowing up before my eyes. Someone I trusted had broken that bond in an awful way. I remembered all the people who had come alongside me as I grew up, always ready to help, and how I'd worked so hard to earn that generosity. I'd wanted to be that for him. I thought of him as family, and he'd stabbed me in the back.

My friend was understanding and offered his best advice: "Sometimes people make bad choices. You can give someone opportunities, but ultimately, they have to choose to do something great with it. This kid chose poorly, but in this case, he took you down with him. You've got an uphill climb ahead of you, but you get to decide if you're going to do it alone or with Ashley."

He told me the same thing Ashley's email had; I had to decide whether to commit or let her go.

It didn't take me too long to decide what to do. I think if something is meant to be, it'll be, and with everything happening, it seemed obvious that heaven and earth were screaming at me to go home to Ashley as soon as possible. I wasn't sure if it was fair to ask her to be with me as my life seemed to be crumbling around me, but I realized she made my life, and me, better. If she was in, so was I. I had only arrived in the Philippines in August, but I got a plane ticket home and surprised Ashley by coming back on Labor Day.

Sure, I'm grateful now that I went home when I did, but at the time, despite being happy to see Ashley and being as sure as I could that what we had was the real deal, I couldn't help but feel defeated coming home to a mess of a business. It seemed like all the work I had done was for nothing.

The good news was I had Ashley; she was right there by my side through all of it. And that was the only good news at the time. Things had to get worse before they'd get better. Ashley was working as a nurse at a long-term care facility, and her hours got massively cut. My business officially went under. With both of us hurting for money in a big way and without the credit to secure my own place, we moved in with her parents that Christmas.

I try to focus on problem-solving rather than wallowing in self-pity. Even though things looked bad, I kept working even harder. The problem was pretty clear cut: bad credit and no money. I knew the way forward, which was a lot more hard work and hours away from home. It meant grinding to make my business viable again. I had two completed rental properties and three properties I needed to remodel, so I put my head down and got busy. Thankfully, although it wasn't the most fun in the world, Ashley was totally on board.

I was grinding from day one. I once worked seven jobs while trying to build my business, but the number of hours I put into my work hit a new level when I returned from the Philippines. I was doing hard physical labor every spare second, saving money in whatever way I could, and trying to find the quickest way to get back on my feet. My friend had some work for me, and I jumped at the opportunity to get more funds.

Of course, working for my friend meant I had fewer hours to pour into recovering my own business. I constantly felt like I was taking one step forward and two steps back. I wanted to be in control of building my future, and I felt conflicted between working to rebuild my business and working for my friend to build up his. I once read a Farrah Gray quote that stuck with me: "Build your own dreams, or someone else will hire you to build theirs." That's exactly what I felt I was doing in these moments—building his dreams instead of my own. But there was no denying that I needed that regular paycheck, and at the time, I didn't have a lot of options. Even though Ashley was back to working solid hours, she wasn't getting paid enough. So, we just kept taking any opportunity to make some extra money.

I reminded myself that this was temporary. I couldn't give up now. Yes, it was a significant and unexpected setback, but every problem has a solution. I would need to make more sacrifices now, but I knew the future payoff would be well worth it.

Sometimes our time of sacrifice lasts longer than we expect it should. Sometimes our season of putting in the hard work and extra hours seems much more challenging than we ever thought we could handle. But it's in these seasons that we are tested, tried, and strengthened. In these moments, we build up a steadfastness that helps us to carry on, finding the best in every situation.

I could quickly see that the woman who stuck around through all of this was someone special, and because of that, I didn't wait too long to put a ring on it. Ashley and I got engaged on March 28, 2015, and by that summer, we managed to get our first house together. Of course, we were far from caught up after the dumpster fire that happened when I left the country. So when I say, "We got our first house together," I mean that Ashley bought the house, her parents co-signed, and my name (and still-awful credit) was kept as far away as possible. Our mortgage was less than $600 a month, and we still struggled to make each payment.

Ashley

After Steven proposed to me and we got our first house, we felt we were just on the tail end of our hardship. We kind of had to be. We were engaged, we had a home, and even though it was a common occurrence that we only had about four bucks in our checking account, God somehow managed to provide. Every day Steven would spend hours killing himself to remodel a house, and every night he would make calls to ensure his renters were happy and cared for. We'd think, "This is hard now, but next year is totally going to be our year. We're almost there. This time next year, we'll finally be able to breathe."

With a feeling of hopefulness for the future, we'd put in those long hours. We'd do everything we could, not so we'd suddenly be rich, but so we'd be able to relax. We were putting in the work and holding onto the hope that one day we'd be financially stable enough to work normal hours, have regular date nights, and get our own drinks if we wanted (don't tell anyone, but we definitely still share drinks). We wanted to look at our bank accounts without closing our eyes to pray we had enough money to cover our bills that month.

Because Steven had to work so hard to rebuild his credit, and because we're both a little wild about the things we like to splurge on, we kept our bank accounts separate for quite a long time. Still, sometimes we made purchases that were ... ill-advised, to say the least. And even though we were pinching every penny, those days of working so hard for a shared goal built a crazy amount of trust between us. It had to.

This time of financial hardship could either break us apart or build a significant foundation; there wasn't an option for anything in between. For another couple, our situation could have spelled financial ruin. And I'd be the first to admit that, on paper, our system shouldn't work. Don't get me wrong. We didn't always make the right choices, we didn't always align when it came to what was worth a splurge and what wasn't, and we didn't always come together on big purchases. But as we both worked to build a life we could be genuinely proud of, we always seemed to find a way to come together and never go over the edge. Still, I'm sure it looked outrageous to outsiders.

I cannot tell you how often I'd see Steven looking online at something, smoke practically coming out of his ears as he crunched numbers in his head.

"What are you looking at?"

"Cars," Steven answered.

I frowned, "Do we really need another car?"

Steven shot a look at me over his phone, then returned to crunching numbers. "This car is such a good deal. We can buy it low and make money when we sell it."

"It doesn't matter how good of a deal it is if we can't afford our bills."

"Oh, you mean like the very helpful designer bag you brought home yesterday? You're right. That's really going to make you money someday," Steven said, teasing.

We laughed and joked about how my new Coach handbag was far more helpful than a truck would be before we got serious. He explained that buying the car was important for the business, and I trusted him.

And that was basically how we did it. Sometimes we'd have a sit-down conversation about what we were doing and what we needed to save for. But often, one of us would come home and show off our latest designer purchase. We figured out a way to manage our lives that didn't just work for us—it made us stronger.

Isn't that what relationships are all about? Figuring out what's best for both of you and working out a compromise that is agreeable to both sides? Steven always likes to say that I handle 97 percent of everything, and he handles 3 percent. But within that 3 percent is all of those big, life-altering choices. And that works for us; it always has. But more than just dividing up decision-making after we got engaged, we took the time to be on the same page about our dreams for our life together.

Steven knew a lot about real estate then, so pouring a lot of energy into owning property made sense. I eventually left my job at the long-term care facility and became a nurse for a dermatologist. I considered going back to school to get an additional certification and even put down some money to start the process. But I ultimately realized I was doing what I enjoyed and getting paid well, so I stayed where I was. We didn't need to take on another financial burden for very little (no) financial reward.

We also factored in our considerations outside the business world. Steven and I both wanted a family. That was a big push behind our desire to reach a financially stable place. Neither Steven nor I wanted our kids to have the financial worries that Steven experienced growing up. His family was on food stamps, relied on government assistance programs, and dealt with utility shut-off notices on multiple occasions. He grew up familiar with church compassion funds and shopping at local food pantries.

His parents also struggled to afford common entertainment that many children take for granted, such as going to Chuck E Cheese or the Children's Museum. The fun outings Steven remembers took a little more creativity and a lot less money. His fondest memories include trips to Barnes & Noble to look at *I SPY* books for hours on end or going to a local restaurant to play darts because it only cost 25 cents. Most of the opportunities he got either came from his own hard work or the generosity of others, like his best friend's parents. But despite his parents' inability to provide financially, he never had to question how much his mom and dad loved him. They provided their love unconditionally.

I, however, came from a middle-class family. My dad is Lebanese and grew up in Senegal, West Africa. When he came to America, he and my mom worked hard to build a good life for me and my four siblings, keeping us happy, healthy, and secure. I never had to experience the insecurities, fears, and struggles that Steven's family did. I wanted my children to feel that same stability. I also knew that I ultimately wanted to be a stay-at-home mom. I was all too aware that getting to a place of financial security where that was possible would only become more challenging as the cost of living increased. Not to mention, Steven and I both had the idea of adopting one day and while we didn't know everything involved in adoption at that point, we did know it would cost money.

To build any semblance of the life we wanted—the financial security, the family, and the roles within the household—we had to work hard now.

No matter how far from a fairy tale your life may seem, I think the magic happens when we learn to find contentment within the chaos, in the midst of the "dumpster fire" that we couldn't have prepared for, when all our expectations are thrown out the window. No one's life is perfect, not even ours, but we hang on to the moments that are as good as it gets, and we hope for a better tomorrow while we work hard today. It's not about finding perfection; it's about finding hope for what could be.

While struggling and working hard to recover and build, we both felt hopeful. We had our own place, and although progress was obnoxiously slow, we thought we could see a way out. We felt like we were almost done with all the hard work and non-stop grind and we knew the end was in sight, even if it was still a long way off.

So naturally, it was the perfect time for Steven to buy a whole firehouse without talking to me first, right?

2

BABY, I BOUGHT A FIREHOUSE

Steven

Okay, okay, hang on. Hear me out here. I can feel your judgment through the pages of this book. Was it a good idea for me to buy a firehouse without talking to Ashley first? No. But! Was it a smart investment at just the right time for us? Also, no.

But, hey! The firehouse had just gone up for sale and already had such a renowned reputation in our city. The possibilities of the firehouse inspired everyone, and I think every person that toured it imagined what their lives would look like inside the place. Ashley and I walked through it when it went on the market, both curious about what was inside. I remember her saying it would be a beautiful home someday for whoever bought it. So, I couldn't help thinking, what if we were those people?

Who doesn't think living in a renovated fire station would be awesome? What a unique place to call home. And when we start having children? What a fun place for them to play and grow up, right? It didn't have a fire pole, but it did have a cool spiral staircase and a ton of space to get creative with during the renovation process, my forte. I saw all of its potential, and as someone who restores houses for a living, I knew I was the perfect candidate for this place.

I figured there couldn't be any harm in seeing if I could get a loan and putting in an offer. I wasn't super hopeful. I knew my financial situation. I was slowly but surely starting to rebuild it, but Ashley and I struggled to make ends meet every month. Every time money came in, something seemed to break in one of our rentals, and we'd have to pour that money right back into the business before it could ever touch any of our monthly bills.

I was still spending almost every hour of every day working. Ashley was still working in the dermatologist's office, and our regular "date nights" consisted of Menards trips and the endless excitement of property management and home renovation. With all that stacked against me, I wasn't expecting anything to go in my favor. I figured they'd laugh me right out of the bank, but they didn't. Instead, they granted me the loan.

Okay, so it wasn't the best time to buy an entire firehouse that would need significant restoration. If I'm being honest, it wasn't even a sort-of good time for it. But I knew this firehouse was a once-in-a-lifetime opportunity. It was turned from a functioning firehouse into a home several years ago but had been empty and uncared for. I knew that whoever bought it would fix it up, and by the time it was available to buy again, there was no telling if it would still be in our price range.

Were we far from recovered and financially stable? Absolutely. But did I think buying this house would help us build the life we saw for ourselves in the future? Absolutely! You've got to risk it for the biscuit, right? I'd rather try to get this house and get laughed out of the bank than risk spending the rest of my life wondering what could have been. So really, if you think about it, it's the bank's fault for approving the loan.

But in all seriousness, I saw potential in this house. I could picture future kids running around the atrium. I could picture us having family and friends over for holiday dinners, game nights, and birthdays. I knew it would be a lot of work and that it wasn't the perfect time to buy the place, but life doesn't always present you with opportunities at the perfect time. If you wait until things are picture-perfect, really cool chances will pass you by.

Being a man of faith, I decided that if this was a chance God was offering me, I'd take that step and trust that he would pro-vide for our needs. I knew that didn't mean it would be easy, but I figured if this was where God was leading us, he'd take care of us. Now, that doesn't mean that you should go out and buy a new fire station that hits the market and believe that God will "mirac-ulously" provide the funding. But, I had the skills and experience to make this firehouse an investment worth trusting my gut on. I just hoped Ashley would see it the same way.

I remember the day I decided to tell her. I didn't have the courage to talk face-to-face, so I texted her while she was at work.

"So you know the fire station that we went and toured?"

"Yes…what about it?"

"Well…I might have put an offer in on it."

It took her a minute to reply, "Shut up, Steve. You're lying."

"I swear. I put the offer in last night, and they accepted it."

"Are you serious?" She was waiting for me to turn it into some sort of joke.

"I'm serious." I could tell she was nervous and excited all at the same time. It was a home we both had always dreamt of living in; however, we had no money, and our wedding was only a few weeks away.

Looking for a way to alleviate her stress, I told her I could have the entire place renovated in six months.

Honestly, the fact that Ashley wasn't only on board but didn't make me sleep on the couch for the rest of my life is a testament to our relationship and the type of person she is. Besides, as the old saying goes, "It's always easier to ask for forgiveness for buying a firehouse than to ask for permission." So even though it was a bit unexpected, we started planning and dreaming up ways to restore our firehouse dream home.

Ashley

When I tell people Steven bought a firehouse without talking to me, I usually get a reaction somewhere around shocked and bewildered. I'll be honest; I was also floored when I learned I was the new owner of an old fire station—especially because I'd been inside and seen what it looked like. If you follow us on social media, you've seen parts of our home since we renovated, but I want you to mentally get rid of those images.

If you haven't seen the inside of our house and are picturing something like Mia Thermopolis' firehouse-turned-home in *The*

Princess Diaries, also get that image out of your head. Instead, think more along the lines of the Titanic wreckage. A long time ago, it was beautiful, with gorgeous carpet and pristine white walls, but everything inside had turned green with mold and mildew, and there were puddles of water everywhere, even when it wasn't raining. The ceilings and walls were crumbling, and all around, it was just gross and completely uninhabitable. It needed some serious love.

As Steven said, it had been empty and untended for years, and the place was a piece of work. There was water damage everywhere. Walls had to come down, and there was so much black mold that if you went inside without a mask for more than ten minutes, you'd get a headache. Even though I could see the potential Steven saw, I couldn't help but also see all the work that would go into making the firehouse anything close to a home—especially at a time when we were already working so hard to get Steven's properties renovated and rented out. But in the end, I trusted Steven's confidence that he could get it restored and ready for us in six months, so I buckled up and braced myself for the ride. I could do six months! In marriage, you sometimes have to follow your spouse's lead, even when it looks like you're being led into the dark. Or, in our case, a crumbling, damp, mold-filled building.

The firehouse is a pretty good representation of the life Steven and I have built together. If you look back at how our relationship began, we almost broke up before we even started. It took lots of hard work, patience, and time to build a solid foundation of trust that wouldn't cave in when things got hard. We made mistakes and gave forgiveness to repair the damage. But in the end, we saw and agreed on the end goal of what we were creating together. Like the firehouse, our lives might look cool or interesting and draw some attention from the outside, but understanding the hardships and letdowns we faced may turn people away. What happens behind the scenes is always a lot less glamorous and appealing than the final picture, but that behind-the-scenes work is always what makes that final picture truly beautiful.

And when it came to the firehouse, there certainly was a lot of work in store for us. Did Steven and I wildly underestimate the money and labor needed to make that firehouse even remotely livable? We absolutely did. Did we wildly underestimate the time we'd spend restoring the place? Most certainly. Six months? How adorable. We were chasing potential, and sometimes, potential can be a lot farther ahead than our eyes can see. But we didn't give up.

Do I wish Steven had talked to me first? I mean, sure, it's always nice to get a heads-up when someone is going to buy an entire building. But looking back, I get why Steven did it this way. The house was super well-known in our hometown, and there was massive interest in the property once it was finally back on the market. People constantly tell us how they planned to buy the firehouse but didn't. Steven had to move fast, and he knew it. He didn't want to lose the chance at something that could help us build that future we imagined. So, in July 2016, the same week Steven and I got married, we closed on our massive fixer-upper.

Our wedding was beautiful, and we were so excited to officially start our lives together as husband and wife. But reality set in for us once the "wedding high" passed. We were officially married, which was great, but Steven's business struggled. We were still scraping every dime together to make ends meet thanks to nothing but sheer luck and what we realize now to be a healthy dose of divine intervention. I was trying to balance all our responsibilities and find quality time with my new husband.

While I worked regular hours in the dermatology office, the best way to spend time with Steven was accompanying him to job sites, supply runs, and other property management-related errands—stuff far from the shiny, newlywed phase everyone talks about. The only big difference was that we didn't just have to make ends meet for our home and the business. We also had to embark on the massive job of restoring our new firehouse. Yay us!

Luckily, we weren't alone. My parents are absolute angels and are always ready to help. Not only did they co-sign on our first house, but when it came to restoring the firehouse, they were the first in line to roll up their sleeves and pitch in. They spent hours in that house, health hazards and all, pouring chemicals on the walls to kill the mold and helping us tear down walls, paint, or whatever else we needed to make our fixer-upper firehouse more of a, you know, fixer-upper firehome.

Those days as newlyweds were pretty busy, but we were working hard with the idea that we'd finally be able to breathe any day now. Just a few more days, weeks, months, maybe even years of working hard, and then we could relax. As we worked hard to build our dream home, I had my sights set on having children. We understood that this endeavor would likely add a little more chaos to our lives, but we were ready for it. Plus, I figured it would take a while to become pregnant, so I wanted to start the process a bit early since it might be a long journey. We were not ready for the painful news that proved more shocking than the firehouse purchase and stole any breath I had been holding.

To be fair, I always had a hunch that I would struggle to conceive and might need some medical intervention to get pregnant. My periods were wildly irregular, and I didn't get my first period until I was a senior in high school. I could also go months at a time without getting a period. Before we were ready to start trying, I got on birth control for a few months to regulate my cycle, and it worked! While I knew it was possible I would need to see a fertility specialist, we started trying for a baby anyway.

Besides, I knew you shouldn't see a doctor about fertility issues at my age until you've spent at least a year trying. At that point, I wasn't too worried. My mom had five biological children but had several miscarriages and used fertility medication. The idea of needing medical intervention or even struggling to get pregnant for a bit wasn't as terrifying as it might have been to someone with zero experience in the world of infertility. If my mom could get her body to get with the program, I shouldn't have a problem. My sister wasn't struggling to have kids. Even if I had to get a little help, I was sure I'd be pregnant in no time.

I've never been one to sit and dwell on the bad stuff. Not that I don't let myself feel those feelings, but I don't let them consume me. Maybe it's because I'm the youngest of five, or maybe it's just because that's how my brain works, but I've always been more prone to anger than deep depression. I expect things to go how they're supposed to, and if they don't, I get angry. Maybe I'll get a bit sad and move on once I get the emotions out of my system.

I noticed this pattern when I was younger, and my father was diagnosed with cancer. I was, of course, upset that my dad was sick. I even had to live with extended family for a bit so my mom could be more accessible to my dad when he was in the worst stages of his treatments. But I didn't feel overcome with fear and dread that my dad would die. My mom said he'd be okay, and I believed her. Even though it was hard to see my dad that sick, and it was an incredibly hard road as he went through treatments, I knew my dad was supposed to live and be with us. And mercifully, my father did survive and is still with us today.

I think that experience makes me a good fit for the unique life Steven and I lead. I may have high expectations, but I'm never afraid of a tough road to get where I want. I've struggled with anger when things don't quite go my way, but I think watching my dad fight cancer and survive was formative when dealing with big, life-altering issues like fertility.

I knew I was destined to be a mom. I had a soul-deep desire to stay at home and raise babies. Getting pregnant might be a steep slope, but it wouldn't scare me away from getting what I wanted. Caring for children always came naturally to me, and every time I thought about taking a positive test, getting that first ultrasound, the gender reveal, or the birth, I got excited. I was ready to do whatever it took to start my family. Even though I wasn't a big drinker, I cut out alcohol. I tracked my ovulation and scoured the internet for tips and tricks. Before you email me your favorite wives' tale, myth, urban legend, or hack to get pregnant, know that I've seen them, and Steven and I have tried them. All of them.

After our first month of trying, I couldn't help but hope I'd be pregnant. We've all heard stories of friends and family who had a baby earlier than planned, and they say something like, "We thought it would take a while to get pregnant, but we got pregnant our first month of trying!" It wasn't realistic, but I still couldn't help but hope that would be our story.

And then I got my period.

I remember sitting on the toilet, sobbing my eyes out. I knew I hadn't lost anything, but it didn't stop me from feeling a loss. Despite everything I knew about myself, my body, and the likelihood that I'd struggle to become pregnant, I still hoped something magical would happen. Even though I knew better, I had gotten my hopes up far more than I should have, and I felt destroyed. I couldn't get up from the toilet and couldn't stop sobbing uncontrollably.

Steven knocked softly on the door. "Ashley? Are you okay?"

He opened the door, worried, and I managed to say between gulping breaths, "I got my period. I'm not pregnant."

I remember him kneeling on the bathroom floor with me, providing comfort and reminding me that it would take time. We had to be patient. We were in this together. I knew better than to get my hopes up like that so quickly, but I couldn't help it. I was excited to be a mom. Steven was right, though. It would just take some time. However, it wasn't long before several months had come and gone, every month ending with the same rush of sadness, intense anger at myself and my body, and feelings of frustration and helplessness.

Every month I'd get my period and see negative pregnancy test after negative pregnancy test. I'd cry, yell, and swear if needed, and then I'd have to pick myself up and try again. I was doing whatever I could to increase my odds of conceiving. I would have done anything to see that little pink plus sign.

Still, nothing worked, and as we got toward the end of that first year, Steven and I drifted pretty far from that glowy, coy attitude of, "We're not pregnant yet, but we're trying," and moved into the almost businesslike attitude of, "Steven, it's my fertile window. Drop your pants." Nothing says "the honeymoon's over" quite like having alarms and calendar reminders on your phone to tell you it's time to have sex with your spouse. Despite all that planning, I wasn't getting pregnant. If you've ever struggled with any level of infertility, you know how quickly getting your period can change from "We'll just try again next month!" to a punch in the gut and deep, painful heartbreak.

The one thing I hadn't tried yet was seeing a doctor. That gave me a little hope, and after a year of trying on our own, we got in to see a specialist. The doctor told me I wasn't ovulating—which made sense with my super-rare periods. Almost immediately, I was put on Chlomid. I was familiar with the medication—my mother was put on the same one before she could conceive. Chlomid lowers your body's estrogen production, so your pituitary gland releases a chemical that helps kick off an egg follicle's maturation, hopefully increasing ovulation.

You can talk to your doctor if you want a better, more in-depth explanation, but for the sake of our story, just know it's a drug that addressed my specific fertility issues. I couldn't help but have a lot of faith in it. After all, someone I knew used it successfully, and any doctor will tell you that it's the most widely used infertility drug on the market, with a high success rate.

Being given a new option with highly favorable odds was great news, but the downside was that appointments with an infertility specialist can get expensive quickly. As soon as our visits got coded as infertility visits, we had to start paying everything out of pocket. That meant we were trying to keep our business afloat, restore the firehouse, and find the extra money to pay for tests and doctor visits to get my uterus to start acting like a team player. It was outside our normal budget, and the longer I went without a positive pregnancy test, the more tests the doctor suggested and the more expensive it became.

We chose to have faith and trust that there were other options, avenues, and solutions we could explore. But you can't forget to face the facts, and all of them pointed to financial ruin if we were to keep going down the path we were on.

After that first doctor's bill, I knew we'd have to have an end date for this journey so we wouldn't go completely broke. The added stress, pressure, and deadlines made me feel a little frantic. I couldn't get pregnant on my own, and now it looked like we couldn't afford the treatments and procedures my doctor prescribed. I had a growing pit in my gut as I realized that pregnancy might never be in the cards.

But we weren't ready to throw in the towel just yet. In that first visit, the doctor suggested Steven get tested as well so we could have a complete picture of our fertility needs. Ever the problem-solver, Steven was totally on board and ready to do whatever was needed to figure this out.

Steven

When Ashley and I started trying to get pregnant, I wasn't too stressed about it. Every time she'd get her period, I had the attitude of, "We'll get 'em next time." But I could see how it broke her heart a little more each month. She told me early on that she was worried because of how rarely she had a period. But she seemed pretty confident that a doctor or medication could fix whatever was complicating the process of having kids, so I wasn't stressed. We'd have a baby when we were meant to. I knew this was all a part of God's plan, and it would be okay.

Infertility was never something I'd spent much time thinking about before Ashley, especially on my end. When the doctor suggested I get tested to see if I had any contributing factors, I certainly didn't expect to hear anything bad. I think most guys assume they can have kids if they want to, and I wasn't offended or embarrassed. I know a guy's fertility is often tied up with our society's idea of what a "real man" is, but nothing felt less manly than not doing whatever I could do to be there for my wife. I was committed to figuring out the source of a problem and was just as willing as Ashley to sacrifice time, money, and maybe some physical comfort to start our family. I had no idea what I was in for, but I was ready to go.

For me, the process was straightforward. I had to provide a couple of samples of my sperm to the medical team at the clinic a few weeks apart for testing. But there was a catch. "You don't have to provide the sample here in the clinic, of course," the doctor explained. "However, there is a pretty stringent time limit. If you decide to collect the sample outside the clinic, you'll need to keep your eye on the clock to ensure you can return promptly to give us a viable sample."

I nodded, mentally doing the math in my head. The doctor stepped out to let us talk it through, and I turned to Ashley. "Hear me out," I said. "We have a vacant unit just a few blocks away. That would give us plenty of time to collect the sample and get it back in time!" At the unoccupied property, we were nervous the entire time, knowing that if any of our tenants saw our car out front, they'd have no problem just coming right up to say hello. But we got it done and to the clinic, no problem.

The second time went a little differently.

"Okay, so thinking about traffic and all of that, I'm pretty sure if we hurry, we can collect the sample at home and make it back in just enough time. You won't even have to come back with me. I can just drop it off. What do you think?"

Ashley shrugged. "If you think you can make it without driving like a maniac to get back here."

I promised her that everything would be fine. We got the sample, and I hopped in the car. I wasn't thrilled with how much time was left before my sample would expire, but as long as I didn't run into an accident or anything, I would make it in time. Still, I hit the gas a bit harder to give myself a couple of seconds of cushion.

As I pulled into the parking lot, I noticed I had a more difficult time finding a parking spot than usual. I didn't think much of it as I grabbed my sample and dashed into the clinic lobby. When the door swung open, my stomach dropped. I'd never seen the lobby so full before. The clinic wasn't just for fertility testing, which meant the lobby was never empty, but it seemed that everyone in the city had chosen that precise moment to hit up the clinic. The line to check in was nearly out the door, and people weren't getting checked in quickly. I tried to calm myself, but my panic rose as I watched the time tick by on my phone. Finally, I realized that if I didn't do something soon, my sample would expire right there in line. I looked around me, hoping to see some big, illuminated sign that said something like, "SKIP THE LINE! DROP SAMPLES HERE!"

When I didn't see anything like that, I realized I was out of reasonable options. I didn't care what anyone thought at that point. We just wanted answers, and repeating the sperm collection process felt incredibly frustrating. Without a second thought, I raised my hands in the air, sample in hand. "Hey, guys! Got a sperm sample here, and we're on a time limit! I need to check in, so I need to get up to the front right now!"

Let me tell you, nothing makes a crowd move like telling them you're holding a cup of sperm. Like Moses and the Red Sea, a little path to the sign-in sheet magically opened. I signed in and got our sample submitted for testing just in the nick of time.

I'm not sure how most guys deal with the news that they have a fertility issue because it isn't discussed often. They may feel that infertility is emasculating and something to be ashamed of. It can be a bit of a blow to the ego for some. I know a lot of men struggling with infertility, but they refuse even to get tested, leaving the entire emotional and physical labor of figuring out what's wrong to their wives.

To a certain point, I get the fear of what's holding them back. It's not fun to be told you're the reason your spouse isn't getting pregnant. It's not fun to realize that, even if you're not ready to be a parent yet, you won't have the option. But I knew putting my head in the sand and ignoring the problem wouldn't fix our fertility issues. And I knew that if my body was the issue, or even part of the issue, I'd always wonder if I could have done more to help on my side. Ashley was doing so much to try to get pregnant with her schedule, apps, testing, and reading. I knew I'd never be able to look at myself in the mirror again if I couldn't find the courage to do my part, even if it meant a difficult realization.

When we got the results from my tests back, it was clear that Ashley and I both had fertility issues. Ashley didn't ovulate, and I had a low sperm count. The sperm I did have had low motility, so they didn't travel quickly enough to get to an egg to fertilize it. For context, the doctor told us that typically, guys have about 25 million sperm, and I had about 5 million slow-moving sperm. We realized it didn't matter what Ashley did to get her body to ovulate. If I couldn't do my part in conceiving a child, we'd never get pregnant.

When I learned about my low count and low motility, I knew I had an important decision to make. I could get angry, and I could get depressed. I could lose my sense of self-worth, shut down, and leave my wife to fend for herself when figuring out how to start a family. I'd seen plenty of men in my community do something like that—and I watched their marriages crumble.

Or, I could choose to see myself for who I was. My identity didn't change after hearing those results. I was the only person with the power to make me look like less of a man. I could keep being there for my wife, let her lean on me, be strong where I could, and help her find solutions, or I could hide from it all. The idea of letting my wife walk this journey alone and letting my pride and ego stop us from getting what we wanted felt way less manly than learning I was infertile ever could.

News of infertility is shocking for anyone because it is something you expect your body to be able to do without any effort on your part. You can't ever prepare for shocking news, but you can choose how you react. When I bought the firehouse on a whim, Ashley responded with trust that I would see the project through to the end like I had promised. When I was told that I had infertility issues, I chose to respond similarly, with faith and trust that God still had a plan and he would see it through—whatever that plan entailed.

I decided not to allow the news to break me down. I was still the same man who had walked into the clinic wanting answers. Now that I had them, it was time to problem-solve. I asked the doctor what our options were. The doctor knew Ashley was on Chlomid, and I was told I could have a procedure to remove any obstructions in my scrotal veins that would make it easier for my sperm to move and get to an egg quickly enough to fertilize it.

I'll be honest—it sounded awful. No guy likes to imagine any type of knife or surgical procedure coming close to anywhere down there. But there was a problem, and the doctor had a solution, so I was willing to try it. Plus, by professional confirmation, the chances of us ever getting pregnant without the procedure were slim to none. Whether it's an old firehouse or starting our family, I don't like to fail. I expect to keep moving in faith when opportunities arise. God had a plan. If this was where he was leading us, I'd continue to trust him.

3

PIVOTS AND PROVISIONS

Ashley

Unless you've been told you may never carry a child, you can't understand the emotional toll it has on you. At this point, I tried about three rounds of Chlomid, all unsuccessful. When the doctor suggested Steven get surgery, I was horrified. The procedure sounded awful, but what killed me was that Steven could go through all that pain, and I still might not get pregnant. I saw our bills mounting and thought of the costs of this procedure only burying us further. I thought of the physical pain Steven would be in during recovery. I thought of how that would impact his lifestyle and how hard it would be to get him to sit in one place long enough to heal.

We were barely making ends meet, and the firehouse was an overwhelming project. To Steven's credit, we moved into the firehouse in six months, but it was still far from finished. I just couldn't, in good conscience, add this medical procedure onto all of that when there was still a considerable chance that it wouldn't work.

The obvious other choice was IVF, but the cost was lightyears out of our price range. Steven always likes to talk about how God will provide, but the amount of money we'd need to get IVF started was beyond anything we or our families ever had. And just like Steven's procedure, there was still no guarantee it would work.

"I think we need to call it," I said as we drove home from the Urologist.

"Call it? You mean stop trying to have a baby?"

I was trying hard not to cry. "Yeah, I think it's too much. There's just no guarantee with any of this. If you go through with the surgery, you'll be recovering and in pain, we'll be under mountains of medical debt, and I still might not get pregnant. If we do IVF, we'll be shelling out even more money, and we still might not get pregnant. If any of this were a guarantee, that'd be one thing, but we could put our bodies through hell, spend every penny we have, and still not have a baby. I want to be a mom so badly, but not badly enough to put us both through financial and physical hell for no reward."

Steven always supported my decisions, but he also knew how badly I wanted a family, "Listen, you know I'm up for whatever we have to do to start our family. I'll do anything you want."

"I know."

Steven looked at me and finally nodded. "I'm going to support you in whatever. It's a lot of money but if you want me to do it, I will. And if you want to stop trying, I understand that too."

And that was that. No surgery. No IVF. We'd find another way to start our family or have to accept that we'd never have kids.

While I knew it was the right choice, my soul was crushed. But I wasn't just sad. I was pissed. I was furious with my body. It's not like I was missing one or both ovaries or survived cancer or some devastating injury around my reproductive organs. I was born with all the parts I needed to bear children, but my body wasn't cooperating. My uterus had one job, and it was sleeping on it.

It wasn't fair. I wanted a baby so badly. I wanted to have that moment where I saw a little pink plus sign slowly appear on a pregnancy test. I'd daydream about the ways I could tell Steven I was pregnant. I wanted to see my body grow and change as our baby grew and changed. I wanted to be able to feel my baby kick. I wanted to see the first ultrasound, their little heartbeat blinking on the screen, and to hear the sonogram tech say, "There they are! That's your baby!"

I wanted to relish in the small moments of Steven singing lullabies to my beautiful baby bump. I desperately wanted to celebrate the little life we would bring into the world. I would picture what our baby would look like, half of me and half of Steven. I could see it all so clearly, and every fiber of my being wanted to experience it. It all just felt right, like I was destined for it. But for some reason, Steven and I had bodies that just wouldn't make babies together.

I knew pregnancy wasn't all sunshine and rainbows, but I even wanted to experience the morning sickness, the struggles to breathe, and the pain of childbirth because it would mean I was pregnant. I was growing a baby inside of me, feeling that unique mother-and-child connection you can't experience in any other way. I had so much love to give, and the further I went in my infertility journey, the more I realized I'd probably never have any beautiful moments of carrying a child.

It felt so personally painful. People get pregnant accidentally all the time. People who objectively shouldn't ever become parents have kids. Some parents are given the gift of bearing a child and then choose to abandon, abuse, or mistreat them. Yet here Steven and I were, two people with big hearts who would love a child, care for them, and make sure their every need was taken care of, and we couldn't get pregnant. Steven kept telling me God had a plan, but I didn't share his faith and optimism. It didn't make sense, and it felt cruel. If it was God's plan for me never to have a child while babies would continue being born to parents who didn't want them or never intended to care for them, then God and his "plan" could screw off.

At this point, more and more people knew what we were going through. We didn't take an ad out in the paper or anything, but we've always been open with the people we love. While we were surprised by the number of friends and family who admitted they were also struggling to get pregnant, many people didn't know how to act around us when we talked about our infertility struggles.

When people know you're struggling to conceive but they aren't (or haven't), they usually do one of two things: When you express you're having issues, some will give you their favorite piece of holler wisdom and then tell you what worked for them. They'll tell you things like, "Just enjoy your spouse! Don't let yourself get stressed!" And the really helpful ones will say something like, "Just stop trying. As soon as I stopped trying, I got pregnant." As if it is actual, medically proven advice that you can just trick your body into ovulating.

But the other thing they do (it comes from a good place, I know, but it's awful to be on the receiving end) is remind you of all the terrible things about pregnancy and childbirth. They'll tell you you're lucky not to experience what they did. And I get it. We all just want our pain acknowledged, and women especially are trained to minimize their pain because it's often dismissed. When it comes to carrying and birthing children, there is so much societal pressure for women to love being pregnant and to find pregnancy beautiful and empowering. When a woman doesn't experience that, she can feel ashamed. As a result, many women often keep the rough parts of pregnancy to themselves unless they find those very rare openings to express their pain.

But the thing is, trying comfort a friend struggling with infertility by using it to validate their experiences, they're invalidating their friend's pain by comparing it to something completely different. They are two different pains, two incomparable struggles.

I had many conversations where I told a friend about my fertility struggles, only for them to respond with, "I'm sorry. But hey! On the bright side, you'll never have morning sickness! You're kind of lucky!"

In response I'd always just laugh awkwardly and shrug as I tried to change the subject. I knew they were trying to make me feel better and wanted their pain and struggles validated. But the way it sounded to me in those moments was, "My pain is worse than your pain." Whenever a friend told me I should count myself lucky because they hadn't slept since their baby was born, it felt like a knife in my heart. Didn't they realize that I would give anything to lose sleep from a baby I was able to grow in my womb? Didn't they understand how badly I wanted motherhood—the good, the bad, and the ugly? It was painful to see how many of my friends' attempts to make me feel better were moments when they inadvertently invalidated my pain to validate their own.

When you want to be a parent and find out you're infertile, it feels like control is taken away from you. Among the other feelings of confusion, fear, and grief, there is also the overwhelming feeling of powerlessness over your life. The picture of how you planned your life going is suddenly destroyed. When your friends respond with platitudes, telling you why you're super lucky and should be grateful for those destroyed dreams, it can feel like a slap in the face. Even worse, it doesn't just show you who does and doesn't understand your pain. Rather, it shows how our society hasn't equipped people to be even remotely empathetic in situations they don't understand.

As I dealt with this heartbreak, my friends seemed to get pregnant in waves. I felt like every time I talked to one of my friends, they told me they were pregnant. Of course, I was happy for them, but I'd be lying if I said it also didn't hurt. I'd try to be positive and focus on their joy in that moment, but once I was in the clear, I'd just sob. It felt lonely as everyone around me got to experience the one thing I desperately wanted.

For a while, my best friend and I were trying to get pregnant at the same time. In the beginning, she also struggled. As messed up as this sounds, it was kind of nice to have someone else to talk to and understand this crappy infertility journey. But that all changed on a day I'll never forget.

She and her husband met at our house before our lunch plans, and she had the biggest grin on her face. I knew something was up immediately. "Surprise!" she said as I opened the box she'd handed me.

It was an ultrasound picture. She was pregnant.

My one girlfriend who was walking this infertility journey with me was going to have a baby. My head screamed at me to get excited for her, but my heart felt shattered. I tried to put on my biggest smile for her.

"Oh my gosh! You're pregnant! Girl, I'm so happy for you! When are you due? Tell me everything!"

I did my best to listen and kept my face as bright and cheerful as possible, but I felt devastated.

Just keep smiling, I told myself. *Leave your baggage at the door and be happy for her. She needs you to celebrate with her. She's not trying to hurt you. Don't make this about you.*

I pushed down my urge to cry and scream and focused on celebrating my friend. I hated how jealous and abandoned her news made me feel, and I was worried that I would lose control and ruin this exciting day for her because, despite my pain, I was so happy for her. She wanted to get pregnant as much as I did, and I wanted her to have her baby. But as I listened to her explain how she found out she was pregnant and her plans for this future child, I couldn't help feeling alone and hopeless as I wondered when it would finally be our turn.

Steven and I were trying to decide what we wanted to do and had started talking more about other options. We were both open to the idea of adoption at some point. Adoption wasn't a new idea for us, but it is a big deal, a massive expense, and a long journey. I was still heartbroken over accepting that I'd likely never be able to have a baby on my own, so we weren't sure if we could handle all the emotions that came with adoption. It would take more consideration and financial planning.

When my brother and his wife told me they were expecting, it was a turning point for me. Like all my friends, I was thrilled for him and angry with myself for taking his news personally, but I couldn't help it. It was one more person around me who was getting pregnant. Here I was, spending money I didn't have, using every ounce of my mental, physical, and emotional energy to figure out how I could be a mom, and for everyone else, it seemed to come so easily.

My brother and his wife got pregnant after trying for only one month. I remembered how I felt after my first month of trying to get pregnant, crying in the bathroom after getting my period. That familiar tightness gripped my throat as I imagined what it must have felt like to take a pregnancy test after a month of trying instead of looking for the nearest tampon.

It didn't make sense how my brother and his wife could be expecting after only a month of trying. Why did his part of the gene pool, or any of my other siblings, get a functioning reproductive system, and I didn't? Was I going to spend the rest of my life with this desire to be a mom that would never be met?

My heart was shattered into a million pieces. Feeling directionless and hopeless, I cried harder than I ever had. I completely broke down under the pain and the thought that I might never be a mother. While we'd already discussed the idea of adoption, we began looking into it more seriously that night. Maybe I couldn't carry a child, but we could find a child that needed a home and welcome them into ours.

Steven

Seeing Ashley that heartbroken after hearing the news her brother and his wife were expecting shattered me. I had never seen her look so gutted. I wasn't feeling particularly hopeless when it came to becoming parents, and I wasn't in a rush to have a child. But at that moment, I fully realized Ashley was ready to be a mom as soon as possible, and every day we couldn't take active steps to start our family broke her heart a little more. I didn't even think twice about telling her to look into adoption. The way we were going was only causing her more pain, and we needed to pivot to new possibilities.

I knew a few folks who had adopted or were adopted themselves, so I knew a bit about it. The main thing I took away from all their stories was time. Adoption is a long process. I figured it would take Ashley a while to find an adoption agency and even longer for us to be matched with a birth mom. We put up a goal board in our house to help us stay motivated to pay off debt and save money for adoption. We'd have plenty of time to finish the firehouse and move through the goal points on our board, and when we finally got matched with a birth mom, our finances would be in order, and we'd be all set.

You'd think, as a guy who once bought an entire firehouse on a whim, I'd come to expect things to always move quickly, but our adoption journey was a whole new definition of fast. Ashley found an adoption agency practically overnight, and before we began the process, we had to start putting money down for the agency fees. The ink on our adoption goal board had barely dried.

Still, I trusted God would provide, and we kept moving forward. We announced we were adopting on social media, and one of our family members reposted our announcement on Twitter. Our announcement story went viral, and just like that, the provision we needed came in the most unexpected way.

Neither Ashley nor I had ever gone viral, and we didn't even have Twitter at the time. We're regular people from Iowa. The most fame we had previously experienced came from being recognized as "the people who bought the firehouse." Suddenly, thousands of strangers had their eyes on us and our story. We got a lot of support. Other adoptive families cheered us on, and others struggling with infertility told us they were walking a similar path. We'd get messages from random people around the country wishing us well, and the outpouring of support provided the comfort and encouragement we desperately needed. For a long time, we'd felt alone in our struggles, but now it was clear that we were part of a community that had experienced a similar journey.

But on the way to something good, there will always be resistance. Surprisingly, our announcement of adoption also got a lot of hate. It was our first taste of the dark side of the internet and internet trolls.

When we first went viral, everything was kind of fun. It was exciting to have so many people rooting for us as we began the adoption process. But not long after our announcement went viral, I found Ashley looking at her phone and seeming more upset than I'd seen her in a long time.

"What are you looking at?"

Without looking up, Ashley said, "Comments on our announcement."

"Did someone say something bad? You look upset."

I was as surprised as Ashley was when she explained that most of the comments were nice, but there were quite a few mean comments too. She picked up her phone and handed it to me. I was shocked at what I read. We were just trying to start our family, and we knew there were children out there who needed homes. The thought that we could be the bad guys for wanting to give kids a home when they needed it hadn't even crossed our minds. And yet, the comments were full of hateful accusations.

Just because you can't have children doesn't mean you get to take someone else's. Baby stealers.

How could you just rip a baby from a mother's arms like that?

So selfish and entitled!

Why not just pay for the birth mom to keep the baby?

Maybe God made you infertile for a reason.

Floored, I looked at Ashley. I saw the joy and excitement of our future family completely gone from her face. It made me furious to see how the comments hurt her and made her doubt if we were on the right path. I could see in her eyes that she had taken those insults to heart, and it made me see red. If we ultimately decided we wouldn't adopt, that would have been fine, but I wasn't about to let faceless internet trolls put so much pain and doubt in my wife's heart that she gave up out of misplaced fear or guilt. If adoption wasn't the right move for us, I wanted us to come to that decision, not an internet mob.

"Listen to me, Ashley. You know we're not here to steal anyone's child. We're giving a child a home that needs one."

"Then why are so many people out there telling us how terrible we are? How can this be right if people can think such terrible things about us? Maybe there's something we're not thinking about."

I understood where her doubt was coming from and did my best to curb that fear. "They don't know what they're talking about because they don't know us, okay? Not everyone adopts for the right reasons, but we are. You know we are. There are kids out there who need love, safety, support, and a happy home, and we are ready to provide that to a child who needs it. You will be an amazing mother, and when God is ready to show us the little kiddo we're going to welcome into our family, it will be wonderful. We're not stealing from anyone, and we're doing everything we can to make sure we can be great parents once we match up with a birth mom so she can trust us. We're getting our home ready, and we're going to give them a life full of love and fun and care. We're going to do right by whatever child God brings our way, but we're also going to do right by that child's biological family. You know we will. These commenters don't."

"I don't want to do something that will hurt someone. I just want to be a mom so badly."

I knew how badly she wanted it and how tough and emotional this journey would be, but we knew we were ready. I reminded her how long this road had been and how much time we'd spent exploring options, but most of all, to remember who we were. These people didn't know us, and wasting energy on people who wouldn't have even been interested in hearing our perspective was useless. All we could do was trust where we felt God was leading us and keep the best interest of this child at the forefront. I encouraged her not to let anyone steal our joy and excitement or make her doubt herself and how extraordinary she was.

While she was still anxious, I saw the joy slowly returning. We decided to stop reading the comments on the post and focus on getting our home and our hearts ready for a child whenever one came our way. I fully trusted that God had a plan, even if it wasn't making much sense. As it turned out, that viral announcement led us to our first adoption match. We were connected through a friend whose pregnant sister was planning to place her newborn baby for adoption. After seeing our post online, she entrusted her child to us. It was all happening way faster than we expected, but with the lawyers at the ready, all signs pointed to us becoming parents in a few months.

Ashley

Things can pivot quickly when you're open to the possibilities available. Sometimes we can become so wrapped up in the pain of our present that we're unable to see what could be in store in our future. Likewise, we can become laser-focused on how we think our goals should be met that we can't visualize any other way. But when dealing with infertility, you want to be a mom so badly that you're willing to do whatever it takes.

When we were matched with our first birth mom, it felt like serendipity, but it also followed the trend of our fast-paced, rapidly changing lifestyle.

The birth mom wanted to meet Steven and me, and we dove in headfirst. I started falling in love with this child I had never met. The birth mom and I texted almost every day, and she would constantly reassure me how happy she was with her decision and how excited she was for her baby to be a part of our family. It seemed like our connection was meant to be, and I quickly became very attached despite warnings from my parents and others not to get my hopes up too high since we were still very early in the process.

With her excitement about us raising her baby and the timing, paired with the fact that we had connected through a good friend, it all seemed like destiny. She knew our story and was adamant that I got to experience as much of pregnancy as possible. She insisted that I accompany her to her first doctor's appointment and again to find out the baby's gender. She even asked us to throw a gender reveal party. I was so excited to start my new family, and it felt incredibly special to have the birth mom rooting for us as well.

In a season of pain, God provided unexpected support through a virtual community. Somehow, we always seemed to have just enough money to keep the process going through each milestone, and now we were building a great connection with the mother of our soon-to-be child. There was no doubt that new doors were being opened for us, and it felt good. Until the door we wanted to walk through slammed shut.

4

THE GIFT OF GRIEF

Ashley

The doctor's appointment to find out the baby's gender was scheduled, and I could hardly contain my excitement. Gender reveal party invitations were ready to send out, and I spent hours crafting pink and blue paper floral decorations. I was so eager to celebrate this new little life that I already felt so much love for.

Then everything fell apart. The day before the gender reveal appointment party, I got a text from the birth mother that dropped a bomb on everything.

> *"I'm so sorry you are receiving this in text, I just couldn't find the strength to do this in person, and I've been hesitating this moment. I want you and Steven to know that I meant everything I said, but I've had a very emotional week that's left me doing a lot of soul-searching and questioning my decisions regarding this baby. For this reason, I need to just take a step back and process these feelings to ensure that I am making the*

best decision for myself and my child. I love you both so much and cannot imagine anyone else but you two if I choose adoption. However, in light of all that is stirring in my thoughts right now, I must not ignore these feelings, and I need time to make sure I'm making the best choice for me. Because I value your feelings and do not wish to hurt you, I'm asking that we proceed no further until I am sure of my choice, whatever that may be. To proceed further would only lead to increased heartbreak for us all should I not choose adoption. I have too much respect and love for you both to put you through that. I know this is difficult to hear, and I'm sorry for the pain it's causing you right now. I hope that you both can respect where I'm coming from as well. This is a very big decision that I cannot take lightly. All my love."

I felt like the entire world stopped around me. Everything went silent, and I had tunnel vision as I looked at her text. I tried hard to focus and read the rest but couldn't get past that first sentence. Tears clouded my vision. I was so confused that I didn't know what to say. She had been so certain and so excited just days prior. I thought back to all the times she told me how thankful she was to have chosen us and the texts we exchanged, daydreaming about the little life she would soon welcome into the world. She and I had spent countless days talking about the unique family we wanted to build together, and suddenly, she was done?

I was deeply shaken by the news but also angry. I also had to tell Steven.

With tears streaming down my face, I showed him the text message, "I thought she was certain. I don't understand why this is happening. I just want to be a mom. Why can everyone else get pregnant and not me? What is wrong with me? Why can people who don't want to be parents just get pregnant accidentally? How can God allow abusive parents to bear children, but I can't? How is this fair? What is the point of all of this?"

Steven wrapped his arms around me. "I don't know. It doesn't seem fair at all. You're right. But it's going to be okay. This wasn't our baby, but our baby is coming."

"When? How much longer do I have to wait? How many more times do I have to deal with a broken heart before I get to be a mom?"

"I don't know. But I know that God has a plan."

But I was so angry and hurt I didn't want to hear it, "Screw God's plan!"

For once, Steven didn't know what to say.

"I don't know if I can do this anymore. I can't handle going through this again."

Of course, I always knew the adoption could fall through, but she had sounded so confident that this was what she wanted. She had kept me so present in the process that I assumed she wasn't having second thoughts. I hadn't truly considered that she could back out. I felt totally blindsided, and with one text message, my dreams of becoming a mom came to a devastating end. However, this time, my chance of becoming a mother had felt closer than ever to becoming a reality. Having it ripped away felt like a whole different kind of blow.

Looking back now, I can confidently say that child wasn't ours and was never meant to be ours. The baby's mother wanted to be a parent, and if the birth mother or father is ready to be a parent, that is always best. But at that moment? I was a big bundle of exposed nerves, constantly zipping back and forth from anger, confusion, and a deep sense of hopelessness.

I was jealous of this woman who got to carry a child, and I was angry at God for making me walk this path. If I'm being sincere, I hated her then. I felt stupid, and I had a physical sense of loss. I was mourning an individual I had never met but desperately hoped to meet. I was slowly preparing for a huge change in the form of this new little life, and then in an instant, it was gone. My heart was ready for this precious gift, and the day before I was supposed to find out their gender, all that love and hope was taken from me.

That's the delicate part of adoption. The unknown. It puts you, as the adoptive parent, in a tricky situation. You have to balance the excitement of this potential new child joining your family while guarding your heart if the birth mom decides to parent. Admittedly, I had gotten way too attached way too fast, but I let myself believe that the birth mom was all in, and I didn't let myself factor in the possibility that she could change her mind. If you've walked through the adoption process, you can understand how quickly the eagerness and joy of welcoming a new life into your home can turn to pure grief.

I felt foolish for getting so invested but also devastated that this baby I thought was meant to be our child was meant for someone else. I still wanted to be a mom so badly, but this made me question giving up. It was starting to feel like too much, and I was having a hard time believing that I was strong enough to handle this process.

We later learned that our matched birth mother had done this before—matching with prospective adoptive parents and then keeping the baby. Obviously, that's the birth mother's right. Choosing to place your child for adoption is an incredibly painful, personal choice, and it isn't right for every parent. The last thing we wanted was to take a baby from a mother who wanted them. I wanted to be a mom more than anything, yes. Still, I didn't want to start my family on the back of the coercion or deception placed on another mom to make a decision after labor, when she was probably more vulnerable and exhausted than at any other point in her life.

If I was going to adopt, I wanted the birth mom to be all in. If this mom wanted to keep her baby, I wanted her to keep her baby too. And looking back now, I'm so glad she did. She was meant to be the mother of that baby, not me. That was her child, not mine. I'm so glad she felt empowered to speak up and keep her child, and I wish her and her family the best. But at the moment, all I felt was loss and betrayal. Because it's such a layered topic, I always felt like I had to be careful about expressing my sadness over the failed adoption. Not many people have experienced this situation, which meant I didn't just feel grief; I also felt incredibly alone.

While I can see how our failed plan to adopt gave the child a chance to grow up under the care of its biological mother, I don't want to discount the pain that I felt at that moment and what you might be feeling now as you walk through something similar.

Grief, loss, and sadness are messy and complicated emotions, and we aren't always our best selves as we walk through any kind of trauma. It's hard to see past your pain in those moments, but all you can do is let yourself feel your feelings, process what happened, and do your best to heal and move forward.

At this point, every avenue we tried to use to become parents hadn't worked. It was a cruel, crushing cycle of feeling excited about becoming a parent, realizing it might not happen, having new hope, and then having that new hope dashed again.

I was terrified of going through the adoption process a second time, terrified of getting hurt like that again. With my broken heart on the one hand and the negative words of people on the internet on the other, I started to wonder if it was all a sign that we needed to stop trying to adopt altogether.

Steven

The adoption falling through was hard for both of us, but it was especially rough on Ashley. The pain of the situation was heartbreaking for her because she became attached so quickly, but what made it tougher was that she often felt like she didn't have anyone to talk to about it. She had her parents and me, of course, but when you're hurting, it helps to have a community around you who have walked down a similar road before—people who can understand—and she didn't have that.

Although we had people in our lives that had gone through adoption, few had experienced a failed adoption. And even though I tried my best to be there for Ashley, sometimes I have a hard time remembering that when Ashley brings a problem to me, she's not always looking for a solution. I'm getting better at it every day, but then, I couldn't respond to her pain in the way she wanted or needed. (Fellas, if you've got a wife or girlfriend, working on listening without problem-solving is something I'd highly recommend.)

I knew it didn't help that I didn't feel as heartbroken as she did. I hadn't gotten as attached yet, so even though I was disappointed that it didn't work out, I knew we'd keep waiting for the perfect fit. It was frustrating and hurtful to feel like we'd been led on (especially when we learned she'd done this before), but at the end of the day, I know it's a huge decision and an emotional roller coaster to place your baby for adoption. I always considered the possibility of this arrangement falling through, so I kept my distance emotionally. Because the baby wasn't meant for us, I didn't spend too much time feeling sad. But I know it made Ashley feel more alone when I wasn't with her in her grief.

I also wasn't sure if Ashley would be up for starting the process over. But at the time, I wasn't super worried about what our next steps would be in our adoption journey. For me, the bigger issue at hand was helping Ashley feel better. Initially, I thought the best way to respond to her when she'd tell me about feeling sad or angry was to help her find a solution. If there's a problem, everyone feels better once you've got a solution, right? I quickly realized that she just needed someone to let her vent, hype her up, and let her get out all her feelings without a filter or any interruptions. I started working on being a better listener, but I knew she still needed someone other than me to talk to. After all, I was in the trenches with her, and there's something helpful about talking to someone outside of the situation to let you know your feelings aren't irrational.

Ashley was especially worried about being too honest and too raw with some of her friends who had never gone through an adoption, let alone a failed one. How might those friends judge her if she spoke in anger about the adoption? Ashley is fully aware of how angry she can get, so it makes sense why she rarely felt comfortable talking to people without a filter. Even her parents didn't always understand.

Ashley's parents were huge supporters who never judged either of us. But if Ashley became upset or said something a little too mean while processing her feelings, her dad would try to help by telling her to calm down and speak kinder. However, it made Ashley feel more angry and less open to talking about her pain. As a result, she began distancing herself from relationships and friendships that once meant a lot to her when what she needed most was a safe space to share her feelings.

I was sad that the adoption failed, and the timing felt extra cruel, but the grief took such a toll on Ashley that I wasn't sure if we'd be able to make it through another failed attempt.

Ashley

Whatever kind of loss you're going through, one of the hardest things about healing is letting your feelings out. As a culture, we're just not great at grief. We get uncomfortable when faced with too much raw grief, or we want to soften it or try to fix it so it will go away. But I'm the type of person that needs to feel things. I don't like to keep things bottled in. I needed to get my pain and anger out to heal and determine our next moves. While my mom was always there when I needed her and had experienced her own struggles with fertility, my neighbor, Cari, became another pillar in my support system. Having my anger and sadness reaffirmed by someone who had walked through this struggle more recently and who I could talk to as a friend and peer was a relief.

Cari was different from my other friends because she'd been in my position. There was so much about our situation that she inherently understood without me having to articulate it. Our lives weren't exactly the same. She had biological children but was working through her own hurdles, setbacks, and heartbreaks with secondary infertility, fostering, and adoption. She knew the vast mishmash of emotions I was feeling all too well. She understood better than anyone that sometimes I needed to vent, even if my words were harsh. She understood that I was hurting and needed a safe place to talk without a filter, and she was always ready to back me up and let me know my feelings were valid.

That first failed match broke my heart, but when I'd bring it up to people, especially my friends who had biological children and had never gone through the adoption process, they often wouldn't understand why I was in so much pain. I'm sure they also had trouble wrapping their heads around my grief. After all, I'd never met the baby, I wasn't pregnant, and technically, the baby was never "mine" to begin with. It's hard to feel safe being vulnerable with someone if they don't fully understand what you're going through. It doesn't make that person a bad friend; it just means that you might need to look elsewhere for someone who can relate to your struggle and with whom you can be open with your grief.

When I first opened up to Cari about our infertility struggles, she responded with complete empathy and consolation. At the time, I just knew her as my neighbor, but something made me feel comfortable enough to be honest with her. When she listened and matched my vulnerability by telling me her story about her infertility triumphs and challenges, I knew Cari would become a very special person in my life.

Having someone like Cari to talk to was such a gift. She was the perfect addition to the team of support I had in my mom and Steven. When you're walking through big bouts of grief, you need multiple people to help you heal your heart. Steven was my support and my helper when it came to planning a path forward. My mom was my emotional support and mentor that was always a shoulder to cry on. Cari was someone I could come to and express my entire hurt with zero filters and a charming assortment of swear words. She would just nod that she had been there once too. Steven was getting better at listening to me without trying to solve all of my problems, even though I could tell sometimes he was bursting at the seams with solutions. When I'd get upset, and Steven knew he couldn't help me, he'd call in the reinforcements: my mom and Cari.

Through talking with them and working through my thoughts, I was able to start picking up the pieces of my broken heart. Of course, I needed to heal from deep grief, but having outlets where I could speak as harshly as I needed to was a gift in a tough time. I realized it was okay to feel like this failed adoption was a loss, and I let myself feel that pain as long as I needed to.

I want you to know that your feelings surrounding your specific circumstances of grief are justified for what you've been through. Grief can come with a lot of different emotions. Mine was anger, and maybe yours is sadness, but whatever you feel, it's okay. Once you allow yourself the space to fully express and process your hurt, you can get to a place where healing is possible.

I was still frustrated and angry at my body, and I still didn't understand why I couldn't just get pregnant, but I was working on accepting that we'd just have to try a bit harder when it came to starting our family. I couldn't shake the feeling that I was meant to be a mom. Maybe this adoption didn't work out, but I knew one day we would meet the baby that we were meant to raise.

5

FLAMINGOS

Ashley

After a lot of tears, confusion, anger, and fear, Steven and I finally figured out a way forward. I had worked through my grief of that first failed adoption. Taking the time to understand my feelings and fully express my pain helped me start healing from the trauma I experienced through my infertility struggles. While grief always comes in waves and sometimes catches you off guard, I felt much stronger.

Steven and I had taken an impromptu trip to Florida to be with family, which allowed me to process our recent heartbreaks. Steven and I both realized we weren't ready to give up on the idea that we were meant to be parents. Then we received a voicemail that would change our lives forever. It was from the lawyer we had hired for that first failed adoption.

Ashley and Steven: I am reaching out to you to see whether or not you are open to a possible adoptive placement. I got a telephone call from a professional colleague on the west side of Iowa. She has a birth mother that is coming in on Wednesday. I told her a little bit about you folks, and she is definitely interested in learning more. This birth mother is going to give birth in October to a mixed-race child (African American and Caucasian). The birth father is willing to sign. There are no health issues that we are aware of currently. It sounds like this will be a closed or semi-closed adoptive placement. Please get back to me at your earliest opportunity with your thoughts on whether you might like to proceed with this.

My eyes were the size of dinner plates after listening to her voicemail. A million thoughts went through my brain. I wasn't sure if I had heard our lawyer correctly or if my mind was playing tricks on me.

I instantly picked up the phone and called her back.

"Hello, Ashley. I hope you're doing well. A colleague of mine called looking for potential adoptive parents, and you two were the first people I thought of. This birth mother is much farther along in her pregnancy and seems very motivated to go through with the adoption. If you're up for it, I'd love to start the process of getting you two connected."

I couldn't believe it, but I was excited and quickly agreed to meet her. I still didn't understand why God would put us through the turmoil of our failed adoption, but it seemed that something great was about to happen. I was so excited I felt like I could burst, and I didn't waste any time calling Steven.

"Babe, you'll never guess who I just got off the line with!"

"You're right," Steven said. "Who was it?"

"Our attorney! She has a birth mom who's potentially interested in meeting us."

"That's great, love. Just remember..."

"I know, I know," I said, "Don't get my hopes up too high."

"I just don't want to see you get hurt again, but you know I'll support any decision you make."

I did know that, which is why I'd already agreed to meet her.

Our next step was sending over our profile packet. Adoption agencies have prospective parents fill out a packet meant to serve as an introduction to birth parents looking for adoptive parents for their children. It asks you a lot of questions, from basic stats about your life to more random questions like your favorite animal.

I remember not totally understanding what my favorite animal had to do with my chops as a parent, so I asked the agency rep we were working with.

"You'd be surprised at what avenues to connection birth parents find with prospective adoptive families. It's such a fraught, emotional decision. A lot of birth parents aren't just looking for practical reasons that someone else might make a good parent for their child. Sometimes there are some ineffable things like a general vibe about the parents or something unique that a birth parent might take as a sign that an adoptive parent would be the right fit. You never know what will make an impact on a birth parent, so we like to cover as many bases as possible."

Her answer made a lot of sense and made me consider the question far more deeply than I intended. I'd never put so much weight onto my favorite animal, but now it was important. Steven came to his answer easily: a flamingo.

I rolled my eyes when he told me and went back to thinking about my answers. I didn't think Steven's love for flamingoes would lead us anywhere, but I was wrong. As it turned out, the birth mom that our lawyer matched us with, Makayla, had the same favorite animal as Steven (which, interestingly enough, is also the favorite animal of the person we bought the firehouse from). Makayla took it as a sign that the match was meant to be. Never underestimate the power of sharing the random, small details of your life!

When we discovered Steven and Makayla's shared love of flamingoes, we decided to bring a little stuffed flamingo with us the first time we met. We knew Makayla had other children, so we figured the toy could be for Makayla or her youngest daughter. That silly little flamingo connected us in ways I would never have expected.

I now know that Makayla isn't much of a hugger, but we instantly hugged and cried when we met. We spent hours sitting in the new lawyer's office talking and eating Jimmy John's. Steven had a blast playing with Makayla's little girl.

We clicked instantly and found out later that Makayla had brought her daughter as a test to see if we'd ignore her or try to include her in the day. Our connection with her daughter ultimately made her choose us. From the jump, this match seemed different in all the right ways.

Makayla was already in her third trimester, so the wait between her giving birth and making the adoption official would be much smaller. It also meant that if things fell through, I would have less time to get super attached. I was doing my best to keep my expectations low so I wouldn't be as hurt if things went south, but I couldn't help but start to feel my hope returning. Because she was so far along, she already knew she was having a boy. I tried my best not to paint too many pictures of snuggling with him on the couch as we watched movies or Steven goofing off with him around the atrium of our firehouse. I wouldn't make the same mistake twice—I wouldn't get overly attached until I knew this was our baby. Even though I was terrified of this adoption falling through, we pushed ahead.

I didn't get as close to Makayla as I did with that first birth mom. I kept a healthy distance to make sure she wouldn't feel overly pressured by me constantly hovering over her. Still, we ensured she knew how important it was to us that she was in the baby's life. We told her we wanted an open adoption because we felt it was the best for the child, and the countless stories we read were evidence to back that up. She'd always be our baby's biological mom, and although we'd be his legal parents, we knew she deserved a stable, important part in his life if she wanted it.

Of course, neither Steven nor I knew of the pitfalls for a biological parent that can come from an open adoption. We didn't fully grasp that there are no legal requirements for the adoptive parents to keep contact with the biological parent. We failed to understand the weight of Makayla's decision knowing that we, as adoptive parents, would be legally protected if one day we just decided we wanted to turn that open adoption into a closed one.

It's hard to imagine how uncertain it must feel as a biological parent knowing open adoptions are like a gentleman's agreement and that it's common for adoptive parents to start being open and close things up quickly. Understandably, Makayla was hesitant to agree to an open adoption because she wasn't sure if she could trust us. But she agreed, and we continued moving through the process.

Steven and I won't tell Makayla's story, what led her to choose adoption, her journey to meeting us, and her life after. Don't get me wrong, her story is beautiful, and Makayla is incredibly strong, but that's her story. Instead, we'll just talk about the role she played in our lives and our family, but I will say that from the beginning, she made one thing very clear to us. She constantly told us that she was carrying this baby for us. She may have been dubious about the open adoption and unsure if we'd keep our word, but she made it clear from the day we said we'd adopt her baby that she felt like this baby was meant to be ours.

With all of Makayla's confidence, I couldn't help but also feel confident about the process. I tried to keep myself in check, but a little flame of excitement was growing in me. Even weirder, people were constantly saying that Makayla and I looked alike. I couldn't help but think this was meant to be, and maybe it would work out after all.

Plus, it all seemed very true to form for Steven and me, right? Instead of this years-long process, our next match would come almost immediately and with someone very close to delivery. The firehouse still wasn't finished, and Steven was working crazy hours. I worked as needed at the dermatology office and started working overnights at a long-term care facility. At this point, I was over the constant grind of the rental business that we never seemed to catch up on, so I had begun to spend less and less time on job sites with Steven.

He and my parents bought a few properties together, so I let them handle everything. Stepping away did mean that my time with Steven was even more limited since I wasn't going to properties with him, and when we did hang out, it was still our typical errand runs. We continued desperately trying to claw our way out of debt into a place where we could breathe better and not worry if we'd have enough money to make ends meet.

Steven

The thing about being an adoptive parent is that it's expensive. Even before the baby is born, you're paying for your lawyer's time, the social worker's time, and a portion of the birth mom's living expenses. You might also have to pay for medical expenses depending on the birth mom's insurance situation. Other fees, like those related to the adoption agency or other legal complications, pop up. The Jimmy John's sandwiches we ate when we first met Makayla were the most expensive sandwiches we'd ever had since we ate them in the lawyer's office while our lawyer was on the clock.

While international adoption gets all the press for being expensive (and it is), domestic adoption isn't cheap, either. Of course, we're talking about a child's life here, so I understand why there is so much paperwork and cost involved, but it didn't stop the process from feeling overwhelming.

The adoption is one of the reasons people often assume Ashley and I are rich. We've got the social media thing going on, we've got the cool refurbished firehouse, and we adopted a child. We've got to be loaded, right? While we've just recently started to gain financial stability, we were about as far from rich as anyone could be when we were adopting. We just hustled. A lot. And maybe I refinanced my paid-off work truck and maxed out a few credit cards. But that's why it was intense when things happened quicker than planned. It felt like every dime we earned was either going into a rental property, fixing up our house, or paying for adoption fees, and we'd manage to pay our bills by the grace of God and a bit of help from our Fairy God Parents, Ashley's mom and dad.

Luckily, Ashley's parents moved into the firehouse with us. They had been living in the home Ashley grew up in, but it was getting to be too much for them to care for, so we helped them convert it into a rental. They lived with us and helped fix up the firehouse and cover our massive utility bills. We appreciated the extra help—it was a lifesaver once we matched with Makayla.

Don't get me wrong. Our adoption matches came quickly. However, waiting for an adoption match was all-consuming for Ashley, and finances were the last thing on her mind. After meeting with Makayla, I could see a small glimmer of hope in every new email, phone call, or text message she received. Scrolling through baby-related items on Pinterest became her new favorite hobby, and day-dreaming about nursery details filled in the moments between.

We did our best to keep ourselves as busy as possible, which was easy with our home renovations and rental property up-keep. That's the best way to pass the time while you wait for that life-changing phone call: continue living. Do things that bring you joy either together or by yourself. Enjoy your season of life and cherish those moments as they come because even though you imagine the life you'll have with a baby in your arms, you won't get this time back. You don't want to look at these moments and feel like you missed out on something because you were too busy living in the future or stressing about finances. Things will happen as they're meant to, and that lifetime of joy with a child is worth it.

And even though Ashley and I were trying to keep up our guard around this adoption, it felt more like things would work out with every day that passed, and I wanted to be prepared. Many extenuating circumstances led Makayla to adoption out-side of financial hardships, and it seemed a lot less likely that she'd change her mind one day. She constantly told us how she felt like this baby was ours and was so happy that she could help us start our family. Our interactions before the birth weren't intense, but Ashley and I felt optimistic about our potential fu-ture family, even if it was still cautious excitement. We were as confident as possible that this adoption would go through, so we just tried to keep ourselves distracted from the worries of another failed adoption. Instead, we watched as the due date got closer and closer.

Ashley

Though I've never been pregnant, I've seen my sister and friends go through their pregnancies. When you're pregnant, you get a ton of information about your baby, not to mention the experience of feeling the baby growing inside you. For a biological mom, there are regular doctor's appointments, ultrasounds, and apps to download. You can buy devices to hear the heartbeat at home or go to private studios to get as many 3D ultrasounds as you want. But you don't get that influx of information when you're adopting. It's up to the birth mother what details she gives you. Because our lawyer didn't give me any way to contact Makayla until close to the time of delivery, our interactions were incredibly limited. We were lucky that Makayla found out the gender because, understandably, some birth moms choose not to. I received one ultrasound picture our lawyer sent when she told us about Makayla. That was it. But all those fun check-ups with your doctor where they tell you how big they think the baby is, if you're dilated at all, and any other tidbits of information about your pregnancy? I didn't get to be a part of that.

Sure, I could download a pregnancy app and put in Makayla's due date to follow along, but I didn't get to be involved in those exciting OBGYN appointments where you're secretly hoping they'll tell you to prepare for your baby's arrival at any moment. And because I wasn't the one carrying the baby, I wouldn't get to see my belly change, feel the baby move inside of me, or watch the shape and mobility of my body change as I got more pregnant. The absence of these milestones is one of the things that makes adoption so hard. It's rare for a birth mother to include the adoptive parents in stuff like doctor's appointments. Honestly, it's almost impossible since most adoption matches don't occur in the same city and sometimes not even in the same state.

Adoptive parents usually go through the entire duration of the pregnancy with little to no updates on the baby. I could understand that it was a tough time for Makayla. Even though I wanted more info on how the baby was doing, I didn't want to push too hard. I know lawyers keep contact between the birth mom and the adoptive parents limited for the protection of both parties, and I didn't want to do anything that might make the adoption more painful for Makayla. But it also felt like we were missing out on a lot of beautiful moments that birth moms experience during their pregnancy.

We were very thankful when Makayla allowed us to pick the baby's name. Steven and I had the perfect one picked out at our very first meeting. But because we couldn't connect directly during those first couple of months, our lawyer suggested I send her a letter to hopefully begin building a relationship. I thought it was a great idea, so we wrote a heartfelt letter that included the first and middle names we picked for the baby, explaining why they were special to us. To our delight, when she wrote back, she told us that she loved the first name but asked if we'd consider changing our plans for a middle name and instead name him after his biological brother.

We loved that idea, and it was sweet to see that Makayla was invested enough in the unique little family we would build together. The idea that this little boy would join our family became more real each day. Now that we had agreed on the name Abriel (Ab, pronounced Abe, for short), the blurry picture of our family was getting clearer.

As we moved through the adoption process, both before matching with Makayla and after, we tried to do as much as we could to mimic the milestones most expectant couples get to celebrate. Our adoption announcement was our way of getting to experience a pregnancy announcement. Once our match with Makayla was all but set in stone, we did a photo shoot to announce the match as a way to simulate maternity photos. We even hosted the gender reveal party I desperately dreamed about. But even when we tried to celebrate the journey as much as possible, we had to be conscious of what we could do. Of course, when you're pregnant, it's totally up to you how much information about your pregnancy journey you share. But with adoption, we didn't just have to think about our comfort levels, but the comfort levels of the birth mom and what was legally safe to share publicly.

We struggled with whether we should have a baby shower. Like any expecting family, we needed baby stuff, so a shower was critical to get stocked up on baby goods. But with our failed adoption behind us and the ever-present threat that this adoption could fall through at any time, we struggled over what would be best. Should we have a shower to celebrate this baby, knowing that he might not be destined to join our family? Should we ask family and friends to get us stuff to help us care for a child that might not ever be ours? A lot of adoptive families forgo a shower for that very reason. Still, ultimately, we decided that our practical needs and my desire to have a baby were reason enough to plan a shower. Regardless, I still couldn't shake the feeling that, at a moment's notice, this could all be for nothing.

I know the fear of celebrating a pregnancy is something birth moms feel too. It's why so many expecting moms wait until the end of their first trimester to announce a pregnancy publicly because, after that first trimester, the chance of miscarriage goes way down. But the unique thing that adoptive parents experience, and the thing that makes it hard for adoptive parents to celebrate and invest in their future child's life, is that, unlike pregnancy, there isn't a marker where the parents can take a deep breath and feel some reassurance that they've passed the danger zone. Biological parents get those appointments as the baby grows where they can take a sigh of relief. "The baby's heart is still beating." "The baby's spine is growing correctly." "Their heart is still healthy."

It doesn't mean something tragic can't still happen, but there are these little moments when birth parents can feel more confident that they'll get to hold their baby in their arms. Unfortunately, that relief doesn't exist for adoptive parents. Throughout the pregnancy, you miss the regular updates on the baby's health and sit on pins and needles, fearing that phone call when you hear the birth mom decides to keep her child. Even after the baby is born, there's a period where you can take the baby home, and the birth mom can still decide she wants her parental rights back. Terrifying, I know.

All these looming factors made deciding what ways were both appropriate and safe for our emotions to celebrate and prepare for Abriel tricky. Everyone around you is well aware of this reality, so as adoptive parents, you don't get as many people checking in on you while you're waiting for the baby to be born. Not carrying a baby meant I missed out on the community support many of my pregnant friends received. I know from watching pregnant women around me that they are constantly asked how they're feeling, how the baby is doing, and what size fruit their pregnancy app says the baby is closest to. They get strangers touching their bellies, they get to grab their spouse's hand and put it on their stomach when the baby kicks, friends and family can talk to the baby, and everyone shares in the growing excitement. But with adoption, it's more of a quiet waiting until everything happens very quickly.

The only good thing about not getting a ton of questions about the pregnancy, for us anyway, is that we never had much to report. As I said, we matched with Makayla late in her pregnancy and weren't given much information after announcing the gender. We didn't have much exciting news for most of the pregnancy. That is until she went into pre-term labor.

Our lawyer called us, and suddenly everything started to feel more real.

"Things are advancing a lot more quickly than we expected. Makalya's gone into pre-term labor, but it looks like the doctors have been able to stop her from progressing. Both Makayla and the baby are fine. However, with all of this happening, it's possible that she could go into labor as early as thirty weeks. As you know, we normally try to be the go-between for communication between you and Makayla. However, because things are moving so quickly and because Makayla wants you to be at the hospital for the birth, I want to be sure you two can get in touch right away and not waste time going through us."

This baby was coming soon, and I was having a hard time not falling more and more in love with this little boy. I had worked so hard to keep a healthy distance between me and Makayla, but this made it harder not to get invested.

She and I began texting a little more regularly. Makayla seemed in good spirits and happy that we would raise her child. She wouldn't send me long texts, but she'd send me stuff to let me know that she was thinking of me and the family Steven and I would build with Abriel.

I'm very happy Abriel is going to get to have you two as parents.

I'm so thankful you two came into my life. I know you'll give Abriel an amazing life.

I know you're going to be a great mother for Abriel, but I hope one day you'll be able to have a biological child of your own. I know how much you want to experience that, and you deserve that.

One day she sent me a picture of Sandra Bullock with her adopted son, saying that is what Abriel and I would be someday. I can't imagine what was going through her mind during the process, but from my point of view, I hoped that the thought of Steven and I raising Abriel, and the love she knew we already had for him, gave her comfort.

Things rarely happen how you might expect, but they work out just how they are supposed to. I never would've expected that our first birth mother would've changed her mind, but she was meant to keep her baby. I made sure I lowered my expectations the next time, but I never would've expected the next match to come so soon. Sure, I would've expected to have more support while awaiting our baby's arrival, like most pregnant women get to experience. Still, we did what we could to make the most of our baby's milestones, and we were able to celebrate with the people that loved us most. I would've loved to know more in the process leading up to the birth of our baby, but we were able to know the gender and give him his name. I held onto these victories as we moved forward. Even though it was not how I had expected them to happen, things were happening, and that was much better than nothing.

After the pre-term labor scare, Makayla followed up with her doctor at weekly appointments, checking her and Abriel's health. Because of the circumstances, Steven and I figured there was a good possibility she could give birth early, so we were always close to the phone. After what felt like a lifetime, I got the call from Makayla. Abriel was about to be on his way into the world. The second I saw her name pop up on my phone, I knew my dream of becoming a mom would finally become a reality.

6

CAREFUL PLANS AND CHAOS

Ashley

The day I got the call, it was the middle of the afternoon, and I was working in the dermatology office. I saw Makayla's name and rushed off to answer her.

I could hear her smiling on the other end of the phone, and I was so excited I felt like I could explode. "It's finally time! My doctor scheduled me for induction tomorrow. You and Steven had better get ready because you're going to be parents tomorrow!"

I couldn't believe it. The moment was finally here! I was about to become a mom. After all of the work, tears, fear, pain, struggle, heartbreak, and setbacks, our baby was about to be born. In the next twenty-four hours, we could potentially be holding our new son in our arms. Just the thought brought joyful tears to my eyes. I couldn't stop smiling as Makayla and I worked out the details of the next day. I was about to experience the best day of my life and couldn't wait. For so long, it seemed like motherhood would never happen for me, and I had worked hard to keep myself calm and a little detached in case Makayla changed her mind, but at that moment, I allowed myself to feel complete and total joy.

After I hung up the phone, I saw my co-workers anxiously waiting on the other side of the door. They all knew what was happening, and they knew if I darted out of a room to answer a call, it probably meant the baby was on the way.

I couldn't contain my excitement when I walked out. "The baby's coming tomorrow!"

The entire team cheered, and all my co-workers surrounded me, hugging me and offering to help in any way they could once Abriel arrived. I felt so loved and supported, and for the first time in my adoption journey, everything glowed.

I couldn't contain myself when I called Steven, either. "Tomorrow's the day!" I blurted out. "We're about to become parents!"

Steven was excited but also shocked. We were going to be parents tomorrow, and it felt a little surreal after waiting and hoping for so long.

We busied ourselves getting things in order so we could leave for a few days and started toward the hospital together as one big happy family, ready to welcome one more. Makayla was giving birth in a city a few hours from us, so Steven, my parents, and I didn't waste much time after I got the call to get out of town.

I could barely sit still on the car ride. None of us could. We were all filled with joy, anticipation, and excitement. After so much trauma, it felt like the pieces to my life were finally falling into place, and I just couldn't stop smiling. For the first time, I could confidently say my son was on his way.

As you probably guessed, none of us slept that night. We were too excited. The next morning, I woke up early, straightened my hair, did my makeup, and put on the perfect comfy but cute outfit I had picked for the hospital. I was ready to go. I had visions of me holding him, looking into his eyes, and finally feeling complete. I looked good, felt good, and knew this would be a beautiful day. My parents came to the hospital with us, and we all waited for Makayla to say it was okay for Steven and me to head back to her room.

When she finally said we could come, Steven and I took the diaper bag we had brought to show her all the cute stuff we had packed for Abriel. We spent all morning with Makayla, talking about her life, the new apartment she was about to move into, and all her exciting plans for the future. The room was practically sparkling from the anticipation and love we were all feeling. Makayla's sisters were there, so we not only got the opportunity to get closer to Makayla but also her sisters. I could see the family we were building together forming in front of my eyes, and I couldn't wait for Abriel to join us.

Makayla loves a plan and made sure she had thought out every detail. Steven and I were set up in the hospital room next to her. She had a detailed plan for what and who she wanted in the room when she was pushing, and she even made sure I had a hospital gown so that as soon as Abriel was born, she could hand him right over to me for skin-to-skin contact. Her labor progressed, and it seemed like everything was going perfectly.

Once she started pushing, Steven, my parents, and I silently waited in our hospital room, trying to listen for the baby's first cries. Because we were right next door and were hardcore eavesdropping, we could hear just about everything happening on the other side of the wall. We could hear people talking and Makayla's straining becoming more intense until a sharp, shrill cry suddenly rose above all of it.

Abriel.

Steven and I hugged instantly, and I did my best to fight off the urge to run into the room. Our hearts were so full, and we were so excited that, finally, our son was here. He was right next door, and we were moments away from the first time we'd ever see his sweet, little face and hold him. Once Makayla was cleaned up, they let us come in. But the joy that was practically bouncing off the walls that morning was gone. It was as if someone had sucked all the air out of the room. The mood became extremely heavy, and we instantly felt like intruders.

We got our first look at Abriel when we walked in, but we were hesitant even to head over there because Makayla was sobbing on the other side of the room. The doctor explained that they were concerned about Abriel's breathing and would have to take him to the NICU to monitor him. The nurse asked if Makayla wanted to hold Abriel before they took him, and she said, "No, that's Steven and Ashley's baby."

Suddenly, the reality of what was happening hit me. This day was so happy for Steven and me as we welcomed this little life into the world and our family. While I always knew it would be a hard day for Makayla, I couldn't wrap my mind around the sheer magnitude of her grief until I saw her sobbing in her hospital bed. Makayla had spent months with this little life growing inside her, knowing she would have to hand him over to someone else to raise. Because she had other kids, she knew that instant connection you have with your baby, and I could see her trying to protect herself and her heart by refusing to hold the baby she had spent months carrying and hours laboring to bring into the world. We had promised Makayla from the start that she could be as present in Abriel's life as she wanted, but I knew she wasn't certain if she could trust us. I could see the pain in her eyes and went to her bedside. "Makayla, this is your baby. You are his mom. If you want to hold him, you hold him. We want you to have this time with him. Don't worry about us right now. We're worried about you. Please hold him if you want."

What was left of her strong façade crumbled as she dissolved into more tears. She nodded and held her arms out for her son. As she held Abriel's tiny body, she wept in a way I'd never seen anyone cry before. There was so much pain, heartbreak, and frustration in her cries, paired with so much love. She let us take some pictures in that moment, but I honestly don't love to look at them because it just brings back memories of the raw pain Makayla was going through. I knew and appreciated the sacrifice Makayla was making. Still, it wasn't until that moment that Steven and I fully understood the immense pain and heartbreak associated with her choice.

When Makayla finally handed Abriel to the doctor, the nurse told us to go with Abriel to the NICU. Makayla was still in recovery and couldn't head up there yet, but the nurses made it clear that we should go with him. Steven and I were in shock, looking at the tear-stained face of this woman who had just undergone an incredible physical feat and was now embarking on an even more painful emotional one. Her pain was incredibly palpable, and all we could think about was trying to comfort her and make that pain go away. We walked in a daze over to our hospital room without saying a word.

My parents anxiously awaited us and heard the commotion next door. I knew they wanted updates, but Steven and I were so overwhelmed that we couldn't say anything. We just walked into the bathroom, sank to the floor, held each other, and sobbed.

Steven and I were worried, scared, and sad about Abriel's breathing issues, but nothing could have prepared us for seeing Makayla after she delivered. We did our best not to overstep any boundaries and let Makayla have the time she needed with her son. Still, watching Makayla's pain, grief, and trauma was heartbreaking.

As we sat on the floor crying, I choked out, "Is this the right thing? Are we doing the right thing?"

Steven nodded. "I think so. Makayla has said over and over how she wants us to raise Abriel. I just don't think I was prepared for how emotional this part would be."

"She's devastated, and I don't know the right thing to do."

Grabbing my hands, Steven said, "We'll get through this. We'll let Makayla set the pace here, and we'll be sure she's got everything she needs to feel comfortable. This is going to be hard, but we're building a family here. We need to support Makayla and make sure she knows we're not going to keep Abriel from her."

Even though I wasn't prepared for how acute Makayla's pain would be, Steven was right. She was a part of our family now, so we would support her however we could.

Adoption can be beautiful, and the idea of taking in a child who doesn't have a family or can't stay with their family is a life-changing example of love. But often, the pain of the birth parents is glossed over or ignored entirely. Sure, there are birth parents who simply abandon their children. Still, the reality of adoption usually means one or both birth parents agonize over the decision to place their child with another family.

Worse yet, some birth parents can find themselves in situations where a partner, their parents, or an authority figure manipulates or coerces them into adoption. Adoption is a "beauty from ashes" situation, but that cliché gets used so much that I think we forget that the heart of the phrase implies something is destroyed, and somehow, something beautiful springs from that pain. Even though we love Abriel, are happy he's in our family, and are eternally grateful for Makayla's sacrifice, we wouldn't be doing this story justice if we didn't spend a moment acknowledging the pain our family was born from.

At the end of the day, an adoptive family forms out of a traumatic event. The hope is that the trauma and pain can be healed and a beautiful life can evolve, but it's not always a given. Makayla knew that. She knew she could only trust that we would do right by her and her son and that we wanted to keep her in our lives. Worse yet, she knew she only had our word to cling to when we promised to give her son the life she felt she couldn't.

I think Abriel being admitted to the NICU amplified Makayla's feelings, alongside the natural heartbreak of placing her child with someone else. When we came into her hospital room after the birth, pain drenched the entire room. She was inconsolable, heaving soul-deep sobs. I saw my father while he was in the throes of cancer treatment, sicker than he'd ever been, but it paled in comparison to the pain, anger, and heartbreak on Makayla's face.

A few moments later, a nurse came into our hospital room to make sure we were doing okay and told us Abriel was almost ready to head to the NICU. As we waited, we ran into Makayla's sisters, and they instantly scooped Steven and me into a big hug. I think they could tell we were starting to wonder if anything good could come out of something that caused someone so much pain and if this was the right choice for Makayla. They looked into our eyes and said, "We know Makayla picked the right people to raise Abriel. I know this is hard, and it's hard to see her in so much pain, but there is a reason for everything."

We knew adopting a child was a big responsibility, and we weren't taking it on lightly. Makayla was doing something super-human by making this choice, and we were outrageously grateful for her sacrifice. But none of us, Makayla included, fully grasped what she would have to endure. To look at his chubby little cheeks, adorable little nose, gorgeous brown eyes, to mark the physical resemblance to herself, and still decide to entrust him to us. Worse yet, to have that moment of separation come almost immediately? She was ripping a part of her heart from her body and handing it over to us.

The deep pain was screaming through each of her sobs and staring coldly at us through her tear-filled eyes.

At the NICU, we couldn't hold him for a few hours until they did some tests. I stood over his tiny body in that incubator and couldn't stop crying. Neither of us could. All I could think about was people's comments online when we first announced our adoption plans.

Baby-stealer.

Monster.

Selfish.

Cruel.

With the image of Makayla drowning in sorrow in her hospital bed seared into my brain, I couldn't help but worry that this was the wrong move. Maybe we went into this with good intentions, but could anything good come from it? Were we pushing Makayla to do something she didn't want to do? Were we stealing this woman's child? I just wanted to love a baby who needed a home, but how could taking this little boy home with us be the right choice when his birth mother was so in love with him and heartbroken to say goodbye?

At the same time, I was already starting to feel love for that little bundle of squishy cheeks, chubby arms, and black, wispy hair. After putting him through a battery of tests, the doctors kept him in the NICU for several more hours for observation, but Steven and I could finally hold and feed him. We took photos and tried to relish in the first few moments of what it felt like to be a family, even if it had the potential to be short-lived. My parents came up soon after, and they were so excited to hold him for the first time. At this point, Steven and I were both physically and emotionally drained. Steven always insisted that this was a part of God's plan, but I was starting to seriously wonder what the hell God was trying to do here apart from destroying people trying to do the right thing.

Steven

In college, I was in a really serious relationship with a girl. She was attending college several hours away from me, and we didn't get to see each other as much as we liked. It was always a tough balance. Neither of us had a lot of money for gas, but we wanted to be together as much as possible. Whenever we had the time and money available, we'd try to visit each other. This particular time, she came to visit me back in our hometown. I was sick, so she stayed up all night taking care of me. She insisted on leaving around 4:30 am, as she had a long drive back to campus and didn't want to miss her labs. On her way back, she fell asleep at the wheel and passed away at the scene.

I remember getting the call that she was gone. It felt like my entire world was crumbling around me. She wasn't doing anything dangerous or foolhardy, and she wasn't in a war zone. She was just driving to class after visiting her boyfriend. Me. I knew it wasn't directly my fault that she died, but she was tired that day because she had stayed up taking care of me. Her death seemed so random, so chaotic, and so pointless. I have never felt that wildly out of control of my own life. Someone I loved so profoundly was taken from me, and in those last moments of her life, she was alone. I wasn't there to comfort or protect her. It didn't make sense. What was the point of life and loving someone if they could be tragically stolen from you in a random accident?

At that moment, I completely changed my outlook on life. I knew I wouldn't be able to control everything, but I promised myself from that day on that I would do everything in my power to keep the people I loved safe and cared for. I would never let myself feel that deeply for someone ever again until I could be as certain as possible that I could always protect them.

When it came to Makayla and Abriel, I kept myself on guard. I knew there were no guarantees that Abriel would be coming home with us, and even though I got increasingly excited with each passing moment, I was waiting to accept that he was my son. But I know that Ashley and I will never forget seeing Makayla heartbroken after she gave birth and the baby had to be taken to the NICU. Even as someone who tries to control my emotions and focus on problem-solving, I felt a bit overwhelmed.

I knew we weren't stealing Makayla's baby. I knew that. I knew that we were doing everything we could to respect Makayla's boundaries and give her the space she needed. We wouldn't rip the baby from her arms or manipulate her into adoption if she decided to back out. Still, the pain on her face, the frustration, fear, and anger of being in such a difficult situation without having the control she needed to feel a little stable? I got that. Even though I knew we weren't doing anything wrong, I couldn't help but feel a bit like an intruder or that I should be doing something differently to make this easier on her.

I'm a guy, so I don't have any way of understanding carrying and birthing a baby, but I could relate to her pain at that moment. Losing my college girlfriend and Makayla placing her son for adoption are two very different types of pain. However, I understood the feeling of losing someone you love so deeply and for the heartbreak to only feel compounded by the chaos and unfairness of the situation.

Ashley and I cried for a bit. We cried for Makayla, the baby, the unfairness and pain in this world, and our heartbreak. But ultimately, we came to the conclusion that if this was meant to happen, it would work out. And if it didn't work out, even though it would hurt, the last thing we wanted to do was take a baby meant to stay with his birth mother. Makayla didn't really know us, and she didn't know that when we said we wanted her in this baby's life, we meant it. But we knew. She didn't know that we'd move heaven and earth to give this child a beautiful, fun, loving childhood where all his needs were met and he felt safe, loved, and cared for every day. But we knew.

If she decided to go through with the adoption, we'd spend every day making sure we stuck to our word because that's just who Ashley and I are. We just had to figure out how to reassure her that we were those types of people and make sure we meant it when we said that if she passed the baby over to us, it would be far from the last time she'd see him. We also wanted her to know that if she decided to keep her baby, we wouldn't hate her and only wish her and her family the best.

So, we tried to figure out the best way to communicate we were there for her without being overbearing, but before we could make a solid plan for our next move, things started falling apart. It began slowly at first.

Makayla started asking when we'd bring the baby down to her, but the doctor still had to clear him. The nurses promised to bring the baby soon after. In total, he was in the NICU for about six hours. We reminded Makayla that she could come to the NICU if she felt up to it, but she wanted him back in her room. That's when plans started to change. Initially, she had insisted that Abriel would stay overnight in Ashley and my hospital room so we could bond with him, but this night she decided that she wanted Abriel to sleep overnight with her.

As soon as we heard that, I could see the color drain from Ashley's face, and I felt a giant pit in my stomach. Was it happening again? Was another adoption about to fall through? After we had spent hours in the NICU standing over him, holding him, feeding him, and bonding with him? We wanted Makayla to get all the time she needed with Abriel before we took him home, but this was certainly a red flag that she might be having second thoughts.

When the nurse said Makayla was coming to get Abriel, Ashley's mom asked if she wanted to hold the baby one more time before we left. Ashley refused. I could see the answer written all over her face. She could feel the adoption falling apart and knew how attached to Abriel she had already become. She didn't want to hold or bond further with him if Makayla backed out. I had no idea what the right thing to do was, and we had no idea what Makayla was thinking. It was such a helpless, hopeless feeling, and I hated it.

We returned to our hospital room and spent the next several hours in the dark. We didn't hear from any doctors or nurses, and worse yet, we didn't hear anything from Makayla until the next morning. Ashley and I spent the entire night in our room crying over this little baby that we only got to know for a few short hours. We had already fallen in love with him and felt like we were losing him. Of course, we wanted Makayla to keep Abriel if that was what she wanted, but we also wanted to be parents so badly. We had gotten invested, and it seemed like this was the right choice for all of us. We wanted to give Makayla her space to decide what was best, but we were also hurting. We had only just allowed ourselves to start feeling like he was our child. Then it was all being taken away.

Thankfully, the next morning, Makayla asked if we wanted to spend a few hours with the baby. We still felt like intruders, but at least Makayla wanted us to bond with Abriel. If she was going to keep him, we figured she would have just barred us from ever seeing him again. Ashley's parents and I could see some hope coming back into Ashley's eyes, and it seemed like a reason to feel like the adoption would still happen. When Makayla brought him over, we were floored. He had taken his first bath and had been cleaned up, and he looked totally different from when he was first born. He was so cute, and Ashley and I were both in love.

Of course, we wanted to be sure Makayla got the time she wanted, so we'd spend a few hours with Abriel and then pass him back over to Makayla. Whenever Makayla had Abriel, we'd leave the hospital to spend time with family living in the city, shower, get some food, and try to get out of everyone's way. Ashley let Makayla know to text her if she needed anything or just needed rest and wanted us to take Abriel, which usually came in one-to-two-hour chunks.

As sweet as those times were, they were also really stressful. Makayla was right next door, meaning she could hear if he cried. That made Ashley second guess every choice she made, even down to being afraid to change his clothes when he needed a new outfit. She thought if Makayla heard Abriel cry, she'd think we were incompetent. Still, we tried our best to make the most of that time and love on him as best we could.

We were still feeling cautious, but it seemed like things were moving in a positive direction. And then, the plans changed again when a nurse came in to check on Makayla.

When she mentioned that Makayla was recovering well and would soon be discharged, Makayla confirmed that she had seventy-two hours with Abriel here in the hospital. Makayla spiraled into a panic when the nurse informed her they could not allow her to stay past forty-eight hours without a medical necessity.

We found out what was happening when Ashley received a text from Makayla.

They're saying I don't get seventy-two hours with Abriel anymore. I know I was promised another day, and I'm going to take that time. I don't need to do this, so if I can't be respected and get the time I need, I'm leaving and taking Abriel home with me. I just want every last second with him.

Ashley and I felt like we were standing on the edge of a cliff. One false move, and we'd find ourselves in the pit of another failed adoption. On top of everything, we wanted to make sure Makayla had the time she was promised and clearly needed. No matter how carefully things are planned or how much you intend to control the situation, chaos can always remind you that, ultimately, you can't control everything. As humans, we'd much prefer to have control in every situation. But I believe chaos can teach us an important lesson if we let it—trust. At this moment, we had to trust that Makayla would understand our hearts, realize our honesty, and find peace knowing that Abriel would be in good hands. We were given no other option but to trust. Makayla had to wrestle with the feeling of giving up control and handing over her child.

Makayla called her lawyer demanding an explanation or help, making it clear that she was close to calling the adoption off. To her credit, her lawyer tried to help her see reason, but they just weren't hearing one another. She was getting angrier by the second, so Ashley said we would do whatever we needed to ensure that Makayla got the time she needed with Abriel. We weren't sure how we would figure it out, but we promised that if she just worked with us, we'd find some way to ensure she got her time. We didn't want to push her, but we also wanted to figure out a solution to make Makayla feel better and build her trust in us.

The hospital wasn't budging on her discharge time, so we needed another solution. I think at that point, she felt so out of control that the idea of taking Abriel home with her was the only way she could feel like she had the power she needed. On top of that, Makayla had friends who kept encouraging her to keep the baby. They promised they'd help with childcare, bills, and everything else that goes into having a newborn. And this wasn't Makayla's first child; she already had a couple of children. She was no stranger to the newborn phase.

I could see her grasping at whatever she could during such a heartbreaking time. Ashley was blowing up our lawyer's phone, who was out of town on a business trip, trying to figure something out. She was talking to people at the hospital, anyone she could, to find a way for Makayla to stay one more day. But nothing was happening, and I think Makayla was at the end of her rope. If the hospital wasn't going to help her, and if Ashley and I couldn't get anyone to help her, it made sense that she started to think the best option was just to back out altogether.

7

WAVES OF HOPE

Ashley

I received a text from Makayla saying she was too upset, that this was too painful, and she was pretty sure she would just take the baby home and be done with this entire situation. My heart instantly sank. Steven was sitting next to me, and we were both silent.

I didn't want to push her too far, but I realized something important at that moment. Clearly, our lawyers dropped the ball in more ways than one, and now Makayla and I needed to figure this out on our own. We could only get through this if we sat down and worked it out together, starting with getting to know each other. Until then, I had kept Makayla at arm's length and didn't show her the "real" me. It wasn't that I was being disingenuous; I just didn't want to get overly familiar with her too early on and make things harder for her (especially if she realized she needed to back out).

Plus, I wanted to protect my heart, given my last adoption experience. But now, I just wanted her to know who I was. If that would give her any consolation, I wanted to try it. If she wanted to keep the baby, fine, but I wanted her to make that choice knowing as much of the real me as possible. So, holding my breath, I sent her a text asking if I could come over to talk, and she said yes.

We talked for hours in her hospital room. We yelled. We laughed. We cried. We swore. I was able to take the pain and isolation I felt going through the adoption and not having the support and care I wanted from my community to Makayla. I did my best to let her know that I felt her pain, too, and I was empathetic to the heartbreak she was subjecting herself to in order to help us start our family. I did my best to commiserate with her on the unfairness of her life circumstances that she even had to be in this situation in the first place. I reassured her that we could make something beautiful from all this pain. We talked a hearty amount of smack about our lawyers and how they handled this entire situation, and we were able to see a lot of similarities in each other.

I told her about Steven's business, the endless saga of renovating a firehouse that used to look like the inside of a shipwreck, my nursing career, and how hard we'd been working to build a life for a child. I told her about our pasts and how Steven and I pictured our future, and the kind of life we wanted for any children we had. But I didn't just talk about myself. I asked about her family, her life, her feelings about adoption, her fears for her son, her hopes for him, her hopes for herself, and what she needed to feel more control and safety. I told her that whatever she needed, Steven and I would make sure it happened. We were open and honest with one another, and the situation was so raw that we couldn't help but be vulnerable in those moments. And I'm glad we did because it formed a vital foundation of respect and trust.

After talking, I put my hand on her arm. "Makayla, I just want you to know that Steven and I mean it when we say we want you to be a part of our family. We really do. And I know Abriel will be so much better for having you in his life, as well as any of your other relatives that want to be a part of his life. I know adoption isn't ideal, but if you think this is the right call for you, I want you to believe me when I say this won't be the last time you see us or Abriel. We want Abriel's life to be full of love and joy, and we want him to be surrounded by all the people who love him, including his adopted and biological family. I hope you believe me when I say that because I mean it with all of my heart."

"I know you mean it, but you just never know. And even though I was sure this was the right call before, saying goodbye to him feels like ripping a part of my heart out. I don't have any guarantee that you'll keep me in his life, and with the hospital already going back on their word, I'm having trouble trusting anyone right now."

"The hospital and our lawyers might not be willing to give you the full time you were promised," I said, "but Steven and I are. And I hope this helps you trust that we're not lying to you. We will figure out a way to get you that time with Abriel. I'm not sure how we'll do it just yet, but you'll get your seventy-two hours."

Finally, after several hours of talking, we parted ways. As the day wore on, lawyers came to talk through everything in Makayla's hospital room, and she once again asked for her full seventy-two hours with Abriel. They said there was nothing they could do, and she'd be discharged after forty-eight hours. End of story. She was spent, and I could tell.

She threw up her hands. "I can't do this anymore. It's too much, and I'm sick of people telling me one thing and doing another. I'm just going to sign Abriel out myself and take him home."

Steven stepped up, "What if Ashley and I got you a hotel room? We'll pay for it, of course, and you can have that time with Abriel. And it won't be in a hospital, so you won't have to deal with nurses constantly checking on you. What do you think, Makayla?"

Our lawyer immediately interjected, asking for a private word with Steven and me. As soon as we were in the hallway, the lawyer closed the door to Makayla's room behind us and turned to us with a grave face, "I would like to strongly recommend you do not move forward with this plan."

"Why?" I asked. "She just wants the time she was promised."

"Have you considered that you could pay for a hotel room for her, she spends the night, and then you never hear from her again? At that point, there'd be nothing we could do. If she signs Abriel out, the baby is hers until she signs parental rights over to you. She could stay in a hotel and then be out of your life forever."

I had considered it, but we didn't have many options, and no one else offered a solution. She was going to go home with Abriel anyways. So why not extend a bit of trust, work to strengthen our relationship, and make sure she had the time to make a clear-headed decision?

During the adoption process, there can be a lot of unknowns and worrying until everything is said and done. You have to look for signs of hope and hang on to those moments. I wasn't sure what Makayla would do after her evening at the hotel, but I knew we had to start with trust to build a family together.

Our attorney still strongly advised against the hotel room idea, but Makayla and I had built an understanding. She looked at me and said, "You needed me to trust you, and now it's your turn to trust me." And we did trust her. She also ripped our lawyer a new one over all of the miscommunication.

"You all know how painful this process is, and you know how much pressure and stress I'm under right now. I'm trying to decide what is best for my child's future, and you can't even stick to a simple agreement on how long I get to spend with my newborn before I hand him over to live with someone else? I don't know what you think you're doing here, but it isn't helping anyone. You're jerking me around, and it's making me jerk Steven and Ashley around. They're good people and don't deserve this. We are doing our best to make this work. What are you all doing?"

I listened to her dress down the lawyers, trying not to laugh. At that moment, I felt a weird sense of camaraderie with Makayla. She wasn't just yelling at the lawyers because of her pain. She was standing up for us, too. It made it feel like we were united and gave us what we needed to keep going. Then another wave of hope came.

Just before we left the hospital, Makayla signed the birth certificate. She could have put anything on that birth certificate. She could have even put her own last name down while she was still sorting things out. But instead, she wrote out the first and middle name we had chosen together, and she wrote out Evans as his last name—our last name.

While everything was still up in the air, that little piece of paper gave us the confidence to believe, hope, and trust.

As we were on our way out, Makayla stopped us.

"Before we go, you all should take a family photo. You know, the type of pictures other families take when they come home from the hospital with their newborn. You got him such a cute little outfit to head home in, and I don't want you to forget this day."

I smiled, trying not to get too emotional, "We'd love that."

Steven agreed. "Thank you, Makayla. We'd love for you to be in the picture with us. What do you think?"

Makayla laughed, "I just had a baby, Steven. No one needs photo evidence of how I look today. I'll just take the picture instead?"

After Makayla snapped the picture, the hospital set us up with a gift bag of goodies like diapers and formula. Makayla gave us a tip to take all the baby supplies we could from the hospital room and ask for more of whatever we needed. It finally started to feel like we were a team. We were conspiring to make our family work and give this wonderful little boy everything he needed. It felt great. Makayla and I trusted each other. She was standing up for us and giving me tips and tricks, and on top of everything, she put our last name on Abriel's birth certificate.

We paid for Makayla and Abriel to stay overnight in a hotel and told her we hoped she had a meaningful and special time with Abriel. We gave her the car seat we brought and the diaper bag we packed for him and let her take all the baby stuff we had with Abriel to the hotel for the night. Literally and figuratively, we were handing over everything we had when it came to Abriel and trusting that she'd come back to us in the morning.

Even though she didn't have to, Makayla sent us pictures of Abriel and updated us on how he was doing. She even gave him the bottles and the binky we picked out for him because she wanted him to get used to them. It was starting to seem like the worst of it was over.

The next morning, Makayla texted me about the night. She had her one-year-old daughter with her and Abriel, so things were a bit chaotic. It had been a hard night with the two little ones, but she knew God wouldn't give her more than she could handle. My heart stopped as I read. But when she continued, I got to see her beautiful heart.

I think God gave me Abriel to give to you and Steven. I think he blessed me to finally be able to bless someone else as much as others have blessed me.

Her text moved me to tears. I couldn't imagine the emotional roller coaster she was on, and to get that text from her after spending a night with her newborn son felt like such an honor. Slowly but surely, my hope was turning into reality. Not only did it seem like we'd get to be Abriel's parents, but it also seemed like we were forging a special relationship with Abriel's birth mom.

Finally, the time came for us to meet back at the hotel. We helped Makayla take her things from her hotel room, and she pointed out that she had styled Abriel's hair in a faux hawk, just like Steven styled his hair. She told us, "I styled his hair just like Steven's so he can be a soccer player just like him someday." It was such a sweet moment and meant a lot to Steven. Seeing the millions of little ways she found to tell us that she wanted us to raise Abriel and that she was happy she chose us was incredible.

We met with our lawyers in the empty hotel restaurant to review the paperwork. Legally, the lawyers had to read everything aloud that went into Makayla's termination of parental rights and our acceptance of them. While most legal documents are boring, the room was so quiet as she read that you could hear a pin drop. We were all incredibly emotional hearing the lawyer explicitly spell out the rights Makayla was giving up and the ones we would now be responsible for. Walking through something so emotional with the inherent coldness of lawyers and legal documents was a strange experience. Neither Steven and I nor Makayla really knew how to feel about it, so we just sat silently, processing the situation. Finally, we signed the papers, and our lawyers gave us a goodie bag with stuff for Ab to commemorate the city he was born in. That was that.

Abriel had been sitting with Makayla during the entire legal process, but Steven and I wanted to be sure that we didn't just snatch him out of her arms once the ink dried. We told her to take all the time she needed, and we gave her the space to spend those last few moments with Abriel before she handed him over to us. When it seemed like things were starting to drift toward everyone leaving, I went over to Makayla.

My voice shaky, I said, "Can you show me how to buckle Abriel into his car seat, Makayla?"

She smiled. "I'd be happy to. These car seats are always tricky to figure out. It'll take you a few times to really get it down. But you'll get better with time, don't worry."

It was such a beautiful moment. Abriel's birth mom put him into a car seat for me, showing me how to buckle him in safely and entrusting him with me. It felt like a powerful metaphor for the entire process.

I know it's always surreal for new parents to walk out of the hospital after giving birth to their child, but there is something extra weird about taking home a child you didn't conceive. We didn't have nine months to watch my body grow and change, nine months to sit and slowly prepare. Even though we did have the time to get our home, hearts, and life ready for a child, we didn't have that shift in our lifestyle that many parents experience as the mom slows down a bit as she approaches her due date—instead, we experienced a huge lifestyle change overnight. It was wild but also outrageously exciting.

As Makayla drove away from the hotel with her lawyer and we drove away with our new family of three, it was the first time we realized we could really start bonding with Abriel. Finally, he felt like our son. We took him to see his cousin, had a relaxed night with my parents and Steven's family, and relished in the relief that Abriel was with us, and we finally got to experience parenthood. After so much heartache and fear in the hospital, it was nice to breathe a sigh of relief and start working toward this new life. We couldn't head back to Cedar Rapids yet since Makayla wanted us to take Ab to his first doctor's appointment at a local pediatrician's office. Still, even though we weren't spending our first real night together in our home, it felt magical and wonderful. We felt like we could confidently say that we had a son.

Despite how beautiful that first night was, we couldn't totally relax. We had Abriel and were out of the hospital, but we still weren't in the clear. Makayla had four days left to take back her parental rights, and even after everything we had been through, we assumed nothing would happen. But even with waves of hope, the sea remains unpredictable. Our lawyers called us the very next day.

8

STILL DREAMING

Ashley

"Nothing is for sure yet, but Makayla has been having second thoughts going back and forth on everything. I'm not sure if she's going to sign to get her parental rights back. I just wanted to give you all a heads up."

My ears started ringing. I was already so in love with baby Abriel I felt like I had been punched in the gut. I couldn't believe what I was hearing. She was thinking about taking him back? After everything? The hotel, the birth certificate, doing his hair like Steven's, the sweet moment getting him into his car seat? All of that was just for nothing? I could barely wrap my mind around it all.

In a fog, I thanked my lawyer for letting us know and hung up the phone. We knew there was a chance this could happen, even though Makayla seemed to be at peace with the adoption when we left the hotel. But there's a big difference between knowing something is possible and it actually happening.

All I ever wanted was to be a mom. Growing up, I would try to envision what my future husband would look like and how many children he would want. Would they look more like me or like him? How would he react when he found out he was going to be a father? Would he be as excited as I was? I'd imagine what it would feel like after bringing a baby into the world. And once I got married, I would constantly try to imagine what life would be like for Steven and me with the new little life we created. On the one hand, we'd probably be exhausted after countless hours of labor, but on the other hand, we'd be so excited for our friends and family to meet him or her! We'd stay up all night basking in the love of our new little family of three. We knew we would screw up a time or two, but that didn't scare us. We would have so much love to give and each other to lean on as we learned.

I knew giving birth would be hard and postpartum would be anything but a walk in the park, but I also knew I had my husband and our baby by my side. Together, we were going home to start the life I had always dreamed about. Unfortunately, infertility made it seem like that dream could never happen, but we found a glimmer of hope in adoption. For so long, it seemed like our match with Makayla was perfect, and then as quickly as it all started to come together, it seemed like that family I always dreamed of was being snatched away yet again.

Makayla seemed confident about the adoption when she signed our name on the birth certificate. Even though we knew how hard this was, her questioning seemed to come out of left field. We started to cherish Abriel after that first night, believing that he was our own and our dreams were finally becoming a reality. But after hearing from our lawyer, doubt and worry crept back in and made me wonder if Abriel was indeed our son or if we were just going to leave with holes in our hearts.

We still had to take Abriel to his first check-up with his pediatrician, but now with the cloud of Makayla potentially taking Abriel back hanging over our heads, we had no idea how to approach the appointment. We were his adoptive parents, but we weren't yet his legal guardians. If Makayla was going to take him back, we didn't want to mess up his medical records by filling out some initial paperwork wrong. It wasn't clear what the correct insurance was for him—the state, ours, or something else entirely.

It was another reminder from the universe that even though we had started bonding with him, Abriel wasn't officially our son yet. I was trying my best to find a place where I could make it through the next few days without losing my mind from the fear that Makayla would take Abriel back, and I did my best to act as normal as possible. As promised, I sent Makayla pictures whenever she asked, updated her on Abriel, and told her how well he did at his first doctor's visit.

In typical Steven fashion, he decided to buy another car now that we were a family and needed a safe vehicle for our baby if someone other than us needed to take him anywhere. The check took a long time to clear, keeping us from returning home even longer. Not only were we afraid to continue to bond with Abriel (though, at this point, we both were head over heels for him), but we weren't even back in our own home where we could start to figure out a new normal. It felt like everything was out of our control, and while I was relieved at every passing hour that we didn't get the dreaded call from our lawyers, I was continuously holding my breath, waiting for the final blow to land.

I didn't know what else to do then, so I just held Abriel every chance I got. I'd fall asleep with him next to me, which meant if I woke up suddenly at night, I could instantly remind myself that he was still with us. I tried my best to cherish every moment with him before this brief, beautiful glimpse into what it was like to be a mom was taken away. But one night, I held him and sobbed uncontrollably. I didn't want to talk to anyone; I didn't want to go anywhere. I just needed to sit, hold Abriel, and cry. This waiting game was killing me. If she was going to take him back, I wanted it to happen sooner rather than later so I could start to heal rather than love him more and more, only to have to say goodbye. It was a scary and exhausting time on top of the already scary and exhausting time of those first days with a newborn.

Finally, Steven's check cleared for the car, and our lawyer said we were okay to return home if we were ready and they'd call us if something happened. We were relieved to be heading back. I couldn't help but hope the familiar environment would be calming and help us get through the rest of these four days more easily. But almost as soon as we got home, we got a call from our lawyers. Makayla had signed the papers taking her parental rights back, and there was nothing more that we could do.

It was all over. It was late, so our lawyer said we could wait to come back the next day.

She told us to get some sleep and let us know we could figure out a plan in the morning. I felt my heart shatter into a million pieces and broke down in sobs. All my fears were coming true. Despite my efforts to protect myself, I had completely fallen for this little boy. We were so excited and honored to have him and be his parents. All those nights I spent longing for a child, all of those times I wept over his little body, and all those times I fell asleep with him in my arms because I was too afraid I'd wake up and he'd be gone seemed like a bad dream.

It didn't make sense to me. Everything seemed like it was going well upon leaving the hospital.

Makayla seemed so confident. She appeared at peace with everything. I believed our hard work had created a foundation of trust. Yet, her change of heart left me feeling more confused than ever. I looked back at Abriel's little squishy face, and I couldn't even think about not seeing him again. I had worked so hard to keep myself safe from this heartbreak, but here it was again, only a million times worse because I had gotten to meet, hold, and bond with a baby this time. Now I would lose him before I ever really got to know him. I didn't want to have a baby that was meant to be with his birth mother, but this was all starting to feel like a cruel joke at my expense. I wanted the dream-come-true, not the repeating nightmare.

The next morning, we got up in a daze, tried to get ready like usual, and waited to contact our lawyer. Around that time, we started getting random texts from Makayla, making me wonder if she wanted to take Abriel back. She'd say things like, "When my son is older, tell him ..." I would respond by telling her that we meant it when we said we wanted her in Abriel's life so she could tell him herself. But we didn't understand why she'd be saying something like this, having signed her parental rights back like our lawyer said she had.

As I was texting Makayla, our lawyers were talking to us too. They didn't have any advice on what to do next, real updates on the situation, or guidance on where to go from there. They also weren't telling us that we needed to immediately load up the car and head back with Abriel because they were unclear on what Makayla wanted regarding parental rights. If we thought we had been trapped in limbo before, we were in limbo crazy-town at this point. Steven and I were totally on edge because we were heart-broken and utterly confused. I had reached my breaking point.

I contacted our lawyer in Iowa City and laid it all out on the table. "I don't have anything else to lose at this point. I've tried to be honest and extend her trust, but here we are. I can't do this back and forth anymore. If she wants her parental rights back, I want to bring Abriel back and be done with it. I think I'm going to just tell her how I'm feeling. Even if she says she wants him back, I'll know what's going on and can start finding peace and closure."

My lawyer agreed, so, still dreaming for a miracle, I started writing a text message to Makayla. I essentially said that we understood that this was an outrageously hard decision and that if she wanted to raise Abriel herself, we would never deny a mother that right.

But as hard as this was on her, it was also incredibly hard on us.

We were constantly in this cycle of cautious optimism, bonding, and the bottom falling out from under us. If we were going to raise Abriel, we wanted to be able to build that bond, knowing he was meant to be a part of our family. We told her that we meant it when we said we wanted her to be in Abriel's life and we would never go back on our word to have her as an important part of our family. Technically, she still had two more days to get her parental rights back, but I told her I couldn't take another two days of back-and-forth and that I needed to know where she stood. I tried to be patient, knowing it was her youngest daughter's birthday. Although she understood, she said she would get back to us later.

A few hours passed, and we got a call from our lawyer that it was time; we needed to bring Abriel back. To say I was heartbroken was a complete understatement. I felt as though my heart had been ripped out of my chest, and I would never recover this time. My parents were with Abriel in the kitchen, holding back tears. Steven was trying to comfort me while also dealing with his own grief, and I felt like all the life and hope had been completely robbed from me. But I had a job to do, so I sent Makayla a text to keep her updated.

I'm getting into the shower now, but then we'll load up and head over there to bring Abriel back to you. We should get in around eight.

As I was stepping into the shower, I got a phone call from Makayla.

"What are you talking about, bringing him back? Ashley, I don't want you to bring him back. I want you two to raise him.

If you bring Abriel back here, I will make you turn around and go home."

We talked for an hour, both sobbing. I told her that I wanted to respect her decision, and while I wasn't trying to minimize her grief, I needed her to know that I was on this emotional roller-coaster with her and I needed to exit the ride. She had me promise that she would always be able to see Abriel and be a part of his life, and I assured her once again that Steven and I always wanted her to be present and that she would always be his mom. We gave her our word, and that meant a lot to us. As long as she wanted to be involved, I promised her she would always have a seat at our table and an irreplaceable spot in our lives.

After a long, tearful conversation, she said again that she didn't want us to bring Abriel back. She was certain of it. She wanted Steven and I to raise him.

I knew there was probably a mountain and a half of legal stuff that would have to be sorted out, but when she said she didn't want us to bring him back, I felt a jolt of life zap back into me.

Were we finally at the end of this harrowing journey? Was it all ending with this beautiful baby boy joining our family? I excitedly told Steven and my family what was happening and hopped on the phone with our lawyer.

While my dream was slowly coming back to life, Makayla had signed the papers to get her parental rights back. Even if, to this day, what happened when she signed for her rights back was unclear, it happened. We couldn't just toss the contract in the shredder and be done with it. We had to have our lawyers draft additional documents to reverse the reversal of rights. To their credit, they worked tirelessly on making sure they drafted up a document that perfectly outlined and articulated the adoption moving forward. Finally, things were headed in the right direction, but we still had to wait for the documentation to be signed and processed. And we still had forty-eight hours for Makayla to change her mind. I was on pins and needles, trying not to let myself start thinking that something else would go wrong to throw a wrench in the process.

Steven

I felt like I had spent the last week running a marathon. Ashley was completely drained, and I was caught in a weird place of processing my confusion, anger, and grief and trying to be strong for my wife. I could tell this entire experience was slowly crushing Ashley, and I hated that there was nothing I could do to fix it. I knew there had to be a solution here and that Ashley needed me to help hold her up. I didn't let myself give in to frustration, anger, or despair. I promised Ashley we'd get everything sorted out, and I told her I still trusted that God was in control of everything, even though I was starting to wonder why he seemed to be picking on us so much.

It was after Ashley talked with Makayla on the phone that we felt fully recharged. Maybe we weren't going to lose Abriel after all. Makayla did want us to raise him, and even though we could see our legal bill rising before our eyes, we only felt joy and relief in those moments. We couldn't breathe until all the paperwork was finalized, but we hoped and prayed that we had finally found the baby we were meant to raise.

Ashley

About ten minutes before the time expired on Makayla's legal rights decision to keep Abriel, I got a text:

Everything is signed and ready to go. No turning back now. He's all yours, girl.

Finally, for real this time, my dream came true. I was a mom.

9

THE DERECHO

Ashley

After everything we went through to bring Abriel home, there's not a moment we take for granted. However, I won't pretend that every adoptive parent is adopting for the right reasons, that they always have the child's best interest at heart, care for the birth mother's needs, or aren't using a child to heal their infertility trauma. As with anything, nothing is perfect, and it's irresponsible to talk about adoption without calling out the corruption in the adoption industry and how predators can take advantage of frightened birth parents and vulnerable children.

While I know adoption as a whole is far from perfect, I can say that our experience with adoption was beautiful. We have a family now, and our gratitude goes to Makayla and God. But I also don't want to gloss over the truth when sharing our story. Adoption, at its core, comes from deep trauma on the part of the birth parent, adoptive parents, and the adoptee.

Even when you're fundamentally prepared to deal with the pain and trauma (like Steven and I thought we were), nothing can prepare you for experiencing that trauma in person like we did the day Abriel was born. Even as the adoptive parents, if you're adopting due to infertility issues like us, you will have to work through and grieve that you won't be able to carry a baby like you hoped. It won't be easy, and that longing to be pregnant may never go away, but your healing journey is essential. Dealing with that pain has to come before you can deal with the pain an adopted child may go through.

The tricky thing about trauma and grief is that triggers can pop up and suddenly make you feel like you've hit a giant setback in your healing journey.

And while it's easy to focus on our own grief, we can't imagine the turmoil that Makayla went through deciding on adoption, having sweet Abriel grow inside of her, going through the pain of childbirth, and then handing him over to us. Her trauma and the sacrifice she and other birth parents experience has to be recognized.

However, I want adoptive parents to know that you will have to work through some trauma, too. A failed adoption hurts, regardless, but after the first failed adoption and hearing that Makayla had signed to get her parental rights back, I couldn't help but hit rock bottom. I didn't have the luxury of trying for another baby because my body couldn't do it. As for trying to adopt again, and at that point in the adoption process, Steven and I had paid so much money toward adopting this baby—adoption fees, social worker fees, paying for birth mother expenses to help support her through the pregnancy, lawyer fees—that we had too much financial ground to make up before we'd be able to start shelling out tens of thousands of dollars more to try again with another birth parent.

Even if you don't experience the intense back and forth that we did, or an adoption falling through (or looking like it might), those days waiting, constantly holding your breath to see if the birth parent will take back their parental rights, are absolute hell. It makes it feel impossible, dangerous even, to start bonding with your new child because you might lose them. It makes it feel like even more control is being taken from you and that everything in the universe is trying to stop you from becoming a parent. Then, on top of all of that, you feel outrageously guilty because you know that in the middle of those awful feelings, the birth parents are going through something you can't imagine in placing their child.

But through all of that pain, all of that heartbreak, confusion, and frustration can be an incredibly beautiful new beginning. Once I got that text from Makayla saying Abriel was officially our son, I felt a weight lifted off me that gave me the freedom to breathe for the first time in ages. I was so excited about the possibilities for our family, and I felt grateful that I not only got to be the mom of this glorious child but had also gained the support of his biological family. Our newfound family of three was surrounded by so much love, and we were excited to start building our new life together.

I knew that the everyday realities of parenthood and newborn life would smack us upside the head soon enough, but as I stood on the threshold of this new journey and reflected on what we had made it through, I was proud of us. I was proud of Makayla for her selflessness and bravery. I was proud of Steven for being such a strong supporter. I was proud of myself for fighting for my family and standing tall even when I only wanted to lay on the floor and cry (even though I did some of that too). We survived, and I was ready for whatever came next.

You'd think any other obstacle would be a total breeze after all we went through. But it's true what they say about newborns: they are a lot of work. Ask any parent or primary caretaker of a newborn. It's exhausting, emotionally and physically draining, and your entire life changes overnight. Suddenly words like "blowout" and "soft spot" have a totally new meaning. You're expected to bond with this new little life while being terrified you'll do something stupid to damage the poor kid irrevocably. The one advantage I had as an adoptive mother is that my body wasn't trying to heal and physically recover while trying to care for a brand-new baby. Even still, our emotional journey in adopting Abriel was so taxing that Steven and I were recovering from emotional wounds.

We were finally a family, and Steven and I felt confident enough to start bonding and loving our baby. But truth be told, even though babies are wonderful, even though you've prayed and wished for them, the life you led before your child arrived still exists. Once your baby gets here, they find their way into your family, and the world around you keeps moving. All the expectations people had for you still exist. Bills are still due (and more are added to the stack). Work still has to get done. And because Steven owned his business and didn't have a team to cover for him for an extended paternity leave, he had to get back to it quickly.

Before Abriel, I knew that if I wanted to hang out with Steven, I'd have to go to job sites or tag along with him on errands. And while we tried to do that, it wasn't as easy with a newborn. Job sites were typically dirty, and lugging car seats around proved daunting, not to mention the amount of stuff I had to pack up to go somewhere. It just wasn't worth it, so I stopped going as often and stayed home more.

Thankfully, my parents were still living with us, and they were able to help out with the baby.

Steven was genuinely trying to make an effort to come home at decent hours to spend more time with us. The picture-perfect family Steven and I worked hard to build finally began to feel like our reality. Until nine months later when a derecho hit our city. A derecho is a series of incredibly fast-moving thunderstorms with winds that blow as fast (and destructively) as tornadoes, but instead of moving in a circular motion, they just move in straight lines. While tornadoes and hurricanes tend to get more press, derechos can be just as destructive (sometimes more), and this one hit Iowa in 2020, destroying our city and many of our properties. Suddenly I felt like we were back to square one, only this time with a baby.

Steven was getting pulled back into frantic recovery mode, like he was after he returned from the Philippines, trying to rebuild his business from shambles. I loved Steven's drive and his intense desire to do whatever it took to take care of his family, but I started to wonder if this life was sustainable. With him at the properties all day, I didn't want to live like a single parent, and I didn't want to sacrifice family life and a present father for my son in the name of financial success. We had brought Abriel into our home together, promising him two parents that would love, cherish, and protect him for the rest of his life. If his dad couldn't ever be around because of work, were we failing him? More than that, I promised Makayla that Steven and I would work hard to provide for and love Abriel. Were we failing her too?

Never for a second did I think that we made a mistake adopting Abriel, but sometimes I couldn't help but think we were both incredibly naïve about how we thought life would look once Abriel joined our family. Honestly, I think any parent will tell you that you can't fully understand the exhaustion and the toll the long days and short nights truly take on you.

There's no way to fully comprehend how your life will look with a new addition when you've spent so long just having to look out for yourselves. Steven and I thought things would just sort of find a way to work out because that is what things always seemed to do.

But with parenthood, it didn't feel like things were working out. On the contrary, it felt like things were breaking. The harder we both worked, the more strain it put on us. Steven and I were arguing a lot. We were going into debt trying to repair storm damage, and Abriel was missing out on having his father present. With every day getting more demanding, I realized I couldn't live the rest of my life like this. Maybe Steven was right, and one day the business would finally become stable, and he could work less, but for the first time in our marriage, I couldn't see the light at the end of the tunnel. I was still sure it was there, but it was too far away, and I was too tired to keep straining to find it.

Steven

When we brought Abriel home, I was happy to have a son, but I'll be honest, the infant stage wasn't my favorite. It's not that you don't love your baby, but they don't really do anything when they're that small. They just lay there, cry, coo, eat, poop, and sleep. Playing with them isn't much more than peekaboo, and even though I loved getting to hold him, I knew I'd start building that father/son bond with Abriel when he was old enough to talk, play, wrestle, throw a ball, and goof off with me.

Even still, it's not like I didn't want to spend time with my new family. I wanted to be there with Ashley and help her with Abriel. The issue was that our business needed me, also. After the derecho, our tenants needed habitable properties. With that and the added stress of our incoming money being funneled right back out, home life was proving more challenging. If I wanted to be able to go on adventures with my family, if I wanted to be able to give my new son the childhood I always wanted to, I had to work just as hard as I'd been working before Abriel was born. Ashley had always been on board with our crazy schedule and was as aware of our financial state as I was. She knew that this wasn't what I wanted life to look like in the long run, and I guess I assumed she'd be okay with me continuing to work a lot while Abriel was a baby so I could get our life to a more stable place financially.

Don't get me wrong. I hated working those long hours. I'd spend hours and hours and hours pouring literal blood, sweat, and tears into the properties I was working to fix up, and if I managed to get home before Ashley and Abriel went to bed, I'd be too exhausted to be a super involved dad and husband. I knew Ashley wanted me to be around more, and I wanted to more than anything, but I knew I was working to provide for the little boy snoozing in his nursery. It wasn't just a hypothetical family anymore. I also knew Ashley had the help of her parents, so if I couldn't be around as much as I wanted right now, it wasn't like she was totally on her own. It wasn't even close to ideal, but I knew it would be worth it.

Still, I could see it wearing on Ashley, and I felt increasingly guilty every day that I couldn't spend solid time with Abriel. Even though we couldn't horse around, nothing made me happier than making those chubby cheeks turn up in a grin and hearing his infectious laugh. Tensions were high in the house. No one was sleeping, and Ashley and I had very different ideas of what this season of our life would look like. Our expectations weren't being met, and it was starting to feel like we were digging ourselves deeper and deeper into a hole. Our communication had fallen apart, and we argued more than ever. I was tired and harsh, and so was she. It didn't feel like we were working together to build something anymore. Instead, it was like we had two different visions and goals, and we would get angry at each other when those visions would bump up against one another.

We had brought Abriel into our lives to love and raise him together, but that started to feel like an unrealistic goal. Our family life was breaking down, and for the first time in our marriage, we started wondering if we might be better people and parents if we separated. It wasn't something either of us wanted, but we were constantly at each other's throats and miscommunicating. By adopting Abriel, we promised Makayla that her son would have a loving, stable home, and every day it felt like we were drifting farther from that.

That's the tough thing about having kids, adopted or biological. Often, parents see their children as a way to heal their relationships or fix their lives. It's easy to think that once you bring a kid into the picture, you and your spouse will ultimately come together out of a desire to care for the child, which will smooth out all of the roughness of your relationship. And while I do think we had the expectations that bringing a child into our lives would make our work schedules make more sense, give us a different but matched set of priorities, and bring us together simply by existing in our family, we learned pretty quickly that doesn't happen.

It's not a child's job to heal their parents. Sure, there can be a lot of joy in providing the life you dreamed of for your children. I know I feel that when I get to buy Abriel something dumb like a T-Rex costume, and we stomp around the house, pretending to be dinosaurs. Especially for me, who, as a child, accidentally discovered a puzzle hidden on top of the refrigerator, which was the only Christmas present my mom could afford that year, it's incredibly satisfying to give my son a different life—but expecting him to heal any struggles between Ashley and me? That's not his job.

We started to have increasingly harder conversations about what to do next. And it sucked. A lot.

"So, am I going to see you at all today?" Ashley asked over breakfast.

Things had been so tense, and I was making an effort not to get defensive, "I've got a lot on my plate. We need to get these properties fixed. The longer we wait, the more money we're losing."

Ashley threw up her hands, "Do you realize how many years you've been saying that? It's always that we have to just push a little longer, work a little harder. Now I feel like I'm raising an infant on my own. Our son never gets to see his dad, and you're running yourself ragged over a business and never have anything left for Abriel and me. I don't want this to be my life."

"It's hard, but this is how we pay our bills. This is reality right now. I don't know what else to tell you. I'm doing my best."

"You always say you're doing your best, but nothing changes. You spend all your time at your properties, and Abriel and I get whatever's left—if you even have anything left."

Her words stung, "Listen, Ashley, I'm not killing myself at our business for my amusement. I'm trying to make a life where my wife and child don't have to worry about money! I don't know what you think I'm doing all day, but it's not kicking back and relaxing. I'm fighting to keep us afloat, and it'd be great if you could get on board and see all the hard work I'm putting in every day to save our business! I didn't ask for the derecho to hit. I didn't ask for it to destroy so many of our properties. I'm trying to fix what's broken, and I just need you to hang on through this time so I can get us back on our feet!"

Ashley seemed resigned. "I think the thing that's really broken is our marriage. Maybe we aren't as strong as we thought. Maybe we aren't as good together as we are apart."

"What are you saying? Do you think we need to get a divorce? Separate?"

"I don't know, Steven. All I know is I can't take much more of this."

It felt like a punch in the gut. And it wasn't the only time she tossed around the idea of divorcing or separating. It felt like every day was a fight. The pressure I felt at work and life at home seemed to reach explosive levels. We wanted Abriel to have a stable home with two parents, but maybe we couldn't give him that. Maybe we could give him a better life if we were apart.

But the more we talked about separating, the crazier it seemed. Neither of us could picture life without the other, and even though things were hard, we don't give up easily. At the end of the day, we love each other, and even though we know just the right way to get on each other's nerves, we both wanted to be all in when it came to our marriage. So, instead of going through with the separation plan, we decided we would try to fight for the family we wanted.

Fighting for the family we both wanted meant working hard to make more intentional time as a couple and as a family, trying to find ways to reduce my hours at rental properties, and finding a way to make money more sustainably so we could continue giving Abriel the life we wanted him to have. If that meant moving things around, adjusting to each other, and finding what worked and what didn't, we would make it happen.

With every new stage of life, there will be growing pains, healing, and adjustments. Change is often difficult, but when you focus on what you want—for us, that was a stable family—you keep working toward it and don't let anything else get in the way. Love can help you survive even the greatest breaking points.

Ashley and I were building a family. It was big, it was unconventional, but it was full of love. We couldn't just give up on that because we struggled to adapt. We loved our family too much, and at the end of the day, we loved each other too much. So every day, we did what we could to spend more time together and use the strength of love for our family to keep fighting for the life we wanted.

10

HATERS GONNA HATE

Ashley

As Abriel got bigger, he and Steven started getting into more shenanigans. They love to clown around, so I would record their antics and save hundreds of videos on my phone. Sometimes we'd share them on our private Facebook or in family texts, but that was about it. At the time, I was trying to make my way as a fashion blogger/Instagram influencer on the side of my nursing job, and Steven suggested that I create a TikTok account to expand my brand and try stuff outside of fashion.

I wasn't really on board and kept brushing the suggestion off. Then one day, I gave in and started one, mostly out of a desire to have a better place to put all our family videos, not for platform-building purposes. However, as Steven will never let me forget, that TikTok account evolved from a place for friends and family to see our silly content to something that changed our lives forever.

My refusal to start a TikTok account at first was because I didn't understand it. It seemed like a place where a bunch of kids danced and lip-synced to videos, and that wasn't the type of platform I was trying to build. But after the COVID-19 pandemic started, the platform and user demographics changed rapidly. More adults were beginning to use the platform; it was evolving into more than just an app for kids. So, in early 2021, I gave in and started posting on a TikTok account we named Happily Evans Afterr.

I didn't expect it to turn into much of anything, but one of our videos quickly went viral. Abriel loved it when Steven tossed him in the air or let him hang upside down, and a video of Steven holding Abriel upside down by his ankles and lowering him to the ground to pick up a golf ball caught traction on TikTok. Abriel would constantly throw his binky on the ground, hoping that Steven would play "Claw Machine" and Abriel would flip himself over and retrieve it.

The viral video was one we made super quickly, not thinking anyone outside of our family and friends would see it—you know, the people who knew us, Abriel, the kind of parents we were, and the type of family we had. But suddenly, we had the attention of over one million people. And just like our adoption announcement, that many eyes on us meant we had a lot of supporters and a lot of haters. While a lot of them thought our video was cute and silly, some people who stumbled across our video quickly formed their own negative conclusions.

To their credit, a white dad holding his Black kid upside down, "training" him to retrieve stuff for him, might not have looked great without the proper context. Abriel didn't look upset in the video, but he wasn't laughing either, so it wasn't clear that he was having fun (which he most definitely was). Paired with the centuries of racism, slavery, and endangerment of Black babies? Through the lens of a Black viewer with personal and inherited trauma? Sure, a casual observer could view the video and see a few troubling red flags if they didn't look too far beyond it.

Of course, we weren't thinking about making a video for the masses when we uploaded it. We weren't thinking about representing our family in a way that would ingratiate strangers to us.

We were just using our TikTok to make silly family videos. From a super young age, Ab was extremely sociable and always loved the spotlight. He has always enjoyed being in videos with his dad and especially watching them back later. For us, it didn't go much deeper than that, but suddenly we were thrust into this world where our family was being hyper-analyzed for everything, and a lot of times, we were shocked to see what people took issue with.

Unsurprisingly, folks didn't love videos where Steven and Abriel were doing stunts and taking some (carefully monitored) risks. That's pretty par for the course for the internet. But once again, we were faced with people who were very upset that we not only adopted but we adopted a Black baby. At the very start of our adoption journey, we weren't concerned about the race of the child we were going to welcome into our family. When you adopt, you can let the adoption agency know if you have a preference for things like gender or race, but we didn't make any specifications. We figured we'd get matched with the baby that God intended for us, regardless of their gender, race, or physical ability. If they were meant to join our family, we were ready to welcome them with open arms.

We also knew that having a child that was a different race than Steven or me meant we'd have extra responsibilities. We'd have to make sure our son or daughter had role models in their lives that looked like them, and we'd need to make sure they are connected in a meaningful way to their culture. We knew it'd mean we'd have to do some serious learning from whatever racial group our child came from. If they were disabled, we knew we'd have to make accommodations to our home. We might have to learn ASL or get used to lots of doctor visits. But whatever it was, we were ready and knew it would be worth it. When you're adopting a baby in relative anonymity and are suddenly thrust into the spotlight, people don't get to see your work to prepare for whatever child you would be matched with.

Unfortunately, many adoptive parents adopt children from different races, namely white families adopting Black children, and don't put any value on the child's culture. They don't take the time to learn how to do their Black child's hair and care for it properly, they don't make sure to keep their child connected to their Black family and the Black community, they avoid any hard conversations about the racism that exists in America today, and they only honor the culture of the adoptive family. Then, when those children find themselves not fitting in, searching for answers about their culture and birth family, or maybe rejecting their adopted family altogether, the adoptive family essentially kicks them out of the family unit.

Worse yet, there are a lot of studies that show that Black babies are often cheaper to adopt. Of course, adoptions differ from state to state, so the rules and fees are different depending on where you go. But tangible data shows that some adoption agencies charge smaller fees for parents interested in adopting Black babies. For instance, NPR ran a story aptly titled "Six Words: Black Babies Cost Less to Adopt" that said the adoption fees for a white baby were about $35,000, while fees for a Black baby were about $18,000. The article also chillingly explains the difference as "supply and demand." Because our adoption went directly through lawyers, not an adoption agency, we didn't see any adoption fee differences. But because it is a disgusting reality of what happens in many adoption agencies, I can understand why seeing us with Abriel was met with a dubiousness that we could responsibly raise a Black son. Some people assumed we had adopted our son because he was cheaper. Again, while that wasn't our experience, nor did the adoption fees play into welcoming Abriel into our family, I can understand why strangers might make these horrific assumptions about us.

But we had no idea. About any of it.

Obviously, we know racism exists and that people don't always adopt for the right reasons or with the capability to attend to a child's specific needs. We understood that some people wouldn't like that we adopted a Black baby. But we didn't realize how many people would openly speak out against us on social media. As we got more attention on our TikTok, we received more negative comments from people saying we only adopted a Black baby to prove we weren't racist. They rehashed the old classic "baby stealer" and accused us of using our son for clout. They told us that God made us infertile for a reason.

But they didn't see what was happening in our real life, the stuff we weren't posting in our TikTok videos, and it was truly beautiful. We continued to foster and grow our relationship with Makayla and her entire family, planning visits with her family in Iowa and the part of her family that lived in Arizona.

We Facetimed and texted whenever Makayla felt up to it, and we were always her biggest cheerleaders whenever she called to share her accomplishments. Abriel calls her Mama Kayla, and even though he's still a bit too small to understand where babies come from in any context, he knows who his family is—all of it. We love to dote on his siblings whenever we can, and we go on adventures together whenever we can. Makayla's family was and continues to be a vital piece of the puzzle of raising a Black boy who will one day become a Black man who knows where he comes from and is connected to his culture.

Unfortunately, that intense connection with the birth family isn't the norm for adoptive families, and it wasn't something we were showing on our TikTok.

Suddenly, what went from a fun thing for friends and family started to get real traction. We had to ultimately take a step back and decide what we wanted to do with this platform. As our TikTok presence grew, it became more apparent that we could try to make something out of it if we were willing. But at the same time, it meant that we suddenly had to be incredibly aware of everything we posted and said online because so many people were watching, and not everyone was a fan.

The learning curve of going from online anonymity to viral with a growing platform is steep. I always had to be so careful of what I said and remember that I couldn't just throw out a pithy statement because I thought it was funny or made sense with all of the nuance and backstory I knew (but my audience didn't). I learned that the hard way many times, but the worst was probably when I made a post asking our audience if we should try for baby number two when we hit one million followers. I know, I know, I can feel you cringing from the other side of the page, and I'm cringing too. But let me explain.

After Abriel, we tossed around the idea that we'd try IVF for our second child. I knew we could go to Lebanon to see some brilliant doctors who specialized in IVF, which would be a fraction of what it cost in America. Of course, it'd still be pricey, but it would be more accessible. And I figured that once we hit one million followers, we'd start earning a much higher income that would allow us to pay for the travel and treatments.

But this is TikTok, so there weren't enough characters, allotted time, or audience attention span to explain this. Instead of just keeping that to myself, I put up a post with the pithy caption, "Baby #2 at 1 mil?" It floated like a box of rocks with our viewers. I ultimately removed it, but the internet is forever, and the damage was done. Suddenly we had a barrage of people feeling vindicated that we were adopting kids for clout and our entire family unit was solely for internet fame.

I learned a vital lesson that day, but despite how catastrophic it felt, our platform continued to grow right along with people who disliked us. Despite the "haters," the steep learning curve, and the total lack of room for error, a pretty exciting opportunity was forming in front of us, and we couldn't let it fall to the side because we received some nasty comments. So, we kept making videos.

Steven

I'm always quick to tell people that I was the one who pushed Ashley into making our TikTok and making it a family page now that we've experienced the success we have. But I'll be honest. I had no idea our social media presence could become anything on the scale it is for us now. If you've ever had any sort of post go viral or semi-viral, you know things go from zero to sixty in the blink of an eye. You go from hosting something small and focused on the people in your life to taking on the concerns, perspectives, and questions of people you've never met. And the amount of those literal strangers who had no issue seeing one quick video of me and my son goofing around and drawing outrageous conclusions will never cease to amaze me.

I think Ashley and I were both a bit naïve about what being "professionally online" really meant, so when we first started trying to grow our page beyond that first viral post, we tried our best to explain our situation, desires, hopes, and dreams for our son and let people know we weren't monsters taking children away from their rightful families. But social media isn't the place to have a nuanced conversation based in empathy and understanding. We quickly learned that though there were people who could come to see our point of view and soften their hatred toward us, the folks who hated us simply because we were adoptive white parents raising a Black son would always hate us.

You get to a point where you're just repeating yourself to people so worked up in someone else's comment section that they won't listen to what you're trying to tell them. It's a weird place when you realize there is someone (or, in our case, several people) you'll never meet that just hates you. It's a rough realization, and it's one that not everyone can take.

As Ashley and I continued to make videos, we expanded our platform from TikTok to Instagram, and converted her previous fashion content to match our new family content. We started getting brand deals that paid us real money and realized we had a really important decision to make. We had to decide if we were ready to live a life where strangers would not only judge us from afar but would also continuously leave comments reminding us how much they hated us—a life where we'd be tagged in video responses, referenced in posts, and slandered across various other platforms. We had to decide if we thought dealing with all of that was worth continuing to grow our platform or if we were just ready to stop posting altogether and walk away in hopes that the strangers who hated us would go away, too. Because while all of this hate was taking place, something special was happening.

After years of struggling and working myself ragged to make our businesses succeed, we were starting to get to a place where we could feel good financially. We had a bit more money coming in, and the silly social media page I encouraged Ashley to start was becoming a reliable source of income for our family. But better yet, while Ashley's nursing and my property work took us out of the house and away from each other, creating content brought us together.

Sure, sometimes Ashley and I might make a video alone, with just us and a friend, or just us and Abriel, but the content people liked most was the three of us goofing off and having fun together as a family. Our TikTok wasn't just making us money; it was giving us common ground. It helped our marriage because now that it was our "job," we would have to put our arguments and differences aside to get along and shoot content. Finally, my desire for our family to be more financially secure was becoming a reality, and the time together Ashley desperately longed for was happening.

Ultimately, we decided to do what felt right for our family. We weren't going to make everyone happy. We wouldn't always live in a way that everyone would agree with, and we would unintentionally upset a few people along the way. Our goal was and still is to inspire people and build a small space people can turn to for a good laugh and a whole lot of love. After learning more, people began turning to us for advice when adopting kids of a different race.

Using our platform to educate others is important to us. For example, we would have white adoptive parents reach out and ask us questions they were too shy or embarrassed to ask elsewhere or when they didn't have the resources to get an answer about their adopted child. We would then post the question, and our followers on Instagram would reply. No question was a bad question, and our followers are amazing at showing up and giving their advice. We all had the same goals: placing the children's needs first and breaking down racial barriers.

Ultimately, if we were happy, Abriel was cared for, loved, and happy, and Makayla was on board with our choice to post on social media, we would keep going. We'd do our best to block out any noise from people who hated us and create content that brought our family joy. We kept at it, and the opportunities kept getting bigger and bigger. It was impossible to ignore the huge gift this new venture gave me as a father. Being able to bring in money by simply recording my fun with my family was a no-brainer. But I also realized I had missed so much by spending all my time at properties.

Everyone says kids grow up so fast, and it's true. After flipping a lawn mower over on myself and falling off of a roof (from which I suffered a concussion that resulted in me forgetting I was a dad for a short time), I realized that life is too short. Maybe God was telling me it was time to step away from rental properties, start investing in our social media platform, and be more present with my family.

Just like everything else in our lives, God provided in a pretty wild way. Social media by no means made us rich, but we finally found more financial fredom to start enjoying things. We didn't have to worry if getting a soda from McDonald's would overdraft our account or if a full tank of gas was out of the question. I could buy Abriel and myself toys and tell Ashley it was for social media, and she couldn't get upset!

Ashley was able to finally achieve her dream of becoming a stay-at-home mom, and this once-in-a-lifetime opportunity allowed our family to thrive. Most importantly, Abriel loved and still loves being on camera. We get to provide him with a unique outlet to grow and flourish. We always say that if Abriel comes to us one day and says he hates being on camera, we'd never force him. But for now, he loves it, and watching him become more creative and confident is so cool.

It's brought more experiences we had only dreamt about, like meeting professional athletes and attending live events. Ashley and I went to an Orlando Magic game four years earlier and sat in the nosebleed section. But since our social media platform took off, we were able to take Abriel to an Orlando Magic game with dope seats and hang with 6'10" Jonathan Isaac after the game. We got the VIP treatment at Monster Jam, which Abriel loved. We also got ring-side tickets at WWE (which turned out to be Abriel's new obsession, and now he firmly believes he's John Cena). Abriel even made it on ESPN and Sports Center! To say social media has changed our lives would be an understatement.

We don't take these experiences for granted and always re-member where we came from. Clearly, this social media platform was nothing short of a divine gift, and we weren't about to pass that up.

HAPPILY EVER AFTER

Ashley

Our beautiful family story starts in a pretty normal place—swiping right on Tinder. But that simple action set into motion an epic life that neither Steven nor I could have ever imagined was possible. If you'd told me when Steven and I first started dating that one day we'd be working on diverting from our rental business and leaning into our social media platform, I'd have looked at you like you were nuts. But that's what is so beautiful about our story.

While I think our story is extraordinary now, it didn't start as anything particularly remarkable. We were just regular people from Iowa, trying to build a life together. We took opportunities as they fell in our laps, and sometimes we moved too quickly, but ultimately, we made it work. The hardships, pain, and heartbreak we faced led us to experience the most joyful life I ever could have imagined.

With social media, our pattern of moving quickly helped us grow in ways we could have only dreamed about. Once we realized the hate we received paled in comparison to the people we

141

were inspiring, we had zero doubts about our choice to dive in head first. We grew our following on TikTok and YouTube, created a community on Instagram that we now call our Instagram Family, and landed brand deals that paid us shocking amounts of money to make a few quick videos and posts about their products. We were able to do work that didn't require us to spend hours away from home and didn't exhaust us at the end of each day. There was no risk of suffering some work-related injury that might result in one of us forgetting we were a parent. Honestly, it was a win-win!

Even cooler, we could love on people in a way we were never able to before. Steven and I always had a big heart for people, and we have always loved to do whatever we could to help those around us—even to our detriment. Finding an outlet that allows us to connect with other couples experiencing infertility and ex-emplifying the joy that could arise from that pain was a true gift.

Teaching others about adoption and the love it brings to our family sets our hearts on fire. Social media changed our life entirely. It didn't make us rich by any means, and we're still working hard to pay off stuff like Abriel's adoption. However, the financial stability has allowed us to start saving for Abriel's college, provide him with unforgettable experiences, and splurge on frivolous things like indoor slides and actual fire trucks. But maybe that's a story for another time.

I don't think Steven and I ever had a big focus on the specific career that he or I wanted to do for the rest of our lives. Our focus has always been more on the type of life our jobs allowed us to lead. We would have never thought social media could get us there, but with every passing day, we find ourselves constantly amazed at the opportunities it affords us.

That's not to say it's the perfect gig because it is not. We've had to work hard to create boundaries to keep from endlessly scrolling through comments, internalizing every written word, and reminding ourselves that our worth isn't based on follower counts and engagement rates. That we came to our social media success as adults after spending years working to make our way in the world has helped. We went in knowing who we were and not needing the validation that came from a platform. We started this outlet not expecting to get any sort of fame and have grown incredibly aware of its volatile nature. We could wake up tomorrow and lose our entire following, and if that were to happen, we have careers to fall back on, and we'd keep pushing forward. Our social media platform is a tool to give us the life we want and the ability to care for our friends and family however we want. It is not something to provide us with meaning or other direction. If it all disappeared, we'd certainly be sad, but we wouldn't be directionless.

Knowing who you are and having some skills outside of content creation is really important when embarking on any social media or entertainment career. Knowing if you can handle the negativity that will come with any kind of platform is important. Having an exit strategy is also important. We'll always prioritize our mental health, our safety, and the safety and comfort of our son. Steven and I will be ready to walk away if any of those things fall apart.

Why am I telling you all this? Because I think books and stories like ours can sometimes be watered down to "an inspirational story of how a couple turned their infertility and adoption journey into social media fame." And the thing is, if the big hook of our story is that we built a platform on social media, then we've missed the most important part. The most important part of our story is our family. It's the journey we took—the setbacks, the twists, and the turns—to build a beautiful life. It's how we took the days working up a sweat in rental homes, the days crying over another negative pregnancy test, the infertility doctors, the adoption agencies, the fear that we'd never be able to start a family, and turned that into something truly beautiful. We were able to take all of that pain and struggle and use it to build this wonderful family with Abriel, Makayla, and the rest of their family. The real point of our story is the beauty from ashes we found in our life and how we turned our ordinary into something extraordinary. You can also find this in your life if you're willing to get a little creative and roll with the punches God sends your way.

Our lives became extraordinary long before I started our Tik-Tok. If you're out here waiting for a post to go viral, a casting agent to notice you, or for some other path to fame and fortune, you're missing the most important parts of life. When things get hard, it's easy to think about how much better your life would be if you only had a bit more money, were a bit more famous, or had a few more followers. But Steven and I are here to tell you that if you're basing everything on external validation from other people, you'll overlook the joy in everyday life.

We're able to cherish and appreciate our family and social media success so much more because of the work we did before this all took off, and it's also what helps us stay grounded. Steven and I started our story on Tinder, but we took chances and dared to explore what other unique opportunities we could find. We thought outside the box about what our life could look like—sometimes, because we wanted to explore our options, and sometimes, like when it came to starting a family, we had no other choice. Regardless, in doing that, we made the most of every day and fought for the life we wanted.

I don't want to give off the impression that our lives are perfect since starting to find success on social media. We still have our less-than-impressive or not-so-glamorous, real-life moments. We still have rental properties that we're struggling with. Steven and I don't always agree. Being the parents of a toddler can be exhausting, and things don't always go our way. As people who put our lives online, it can be really easy to fall into the trap of living life and creating experiences not to build that family bond but to make grid-worthy photos or the perfect family vacation videos. Keeping that boundary of separating our real life from our social media persona and valuing our family over followers has been key to ensuring we stay present and purposeful in everything we do.

Ultimately, the top priority for me and Steven has always been family. It's what we worked so hard for before we got married and adopted Abriel, and it's why we work so hard now. You've got to fight for your family and work to keep your family unit healthy. The family we've built is beautiful. We're proud of it, and it has brought us such joy that everything else truly pales in comparison, but it took us a long time to get here.

I don't know what your life looks like right now, but whether you're starting a business, walking through infertility, considering entrusting another family to adopt your child, or exploring becoming a social media influencer, always remember what you're working toward and find joy in the journey, no matter how wild it may get. Don't let yourself get caught up and distracted by the not-so-fun stuff that will come along the way. Instead, keep that goal in mind, and work to build a community to support you and push you forward.

Don't be afraid to seize opportunities as they come your way, and don't stop yourself from trying something because you think it isn't the right time.

Obviously, it's good to be diligent and think things through before you act on them, but that's where that community comes into play. Run stuff by them, get a gut check from them, but ultimately realize there will never be a perfect time to take a risk. If you're safe and the opportunity will get you closer to where you want to go, give it a shot. It could be something as big as buying a firehouse without telling your wife (which I strongly discourage you from doing, by the way) or starting a family TikTok, but don't shrug off the opportunity for adventure and new avenues to explore when it crosses your path. Don't let setbacks discourage you or stop you from chasing your goals. If our life has taught us anything, it's that as long as you keep that end goal in mind and have the proper support around you, you can walk through any challenging or painful season and ultimately find a joyfully beautiful life and family full of love and adventure.

You can find your happily ever after, whatever that looks like for you. You've just got to be willing to accept that it may look a little different than you first imagined. In fact, it may look bigger, better, and fuller than you ever dreamed possible.

ACKNOWLEDGEMENTS

To Makayla - no amount of thank you's would ever be enough to share our gratitude for you and the beautiful gift you gave us. We love you beyond measure and we are so happy to call you our family!

To Ashley's parents - thank you for supporting us through every milestone in our lives. We wouldn't be where we are today without you both!

To Scott and Sarah - thank you for being our safe space to allow our marriage to not only succeed, but to transform into the love you see today.

To our agent, Tyler Bertola, and The Fedd Agency - thank you for believing in us and helping bring our story to life in this amazing new way!

To God - for making all things possible through Him.

ANNOUNCEMENT

When we decided to write this book, it was with a full acceptance of our circumstances and that God's plans were ultimately bigger and better than ours ever could be. We'd been blessed beyond belief with Abriel and even though I wanted to be able to carry a child myself more than anything, we'd accepted that God had other plans for us. We wanted to share the story of his faithfulness and love, even in the midst of our heartache.

During the final stages of this book, six years after our fertility journey first started, we were so blessed to find out we were pregnant. Shock is probably the biggest emotion we've been feeling but also an overwhelming sense of joy and gratitude.

This miracle baby is just more evidence of God's faithfulness. We gave it all to Him and He delivered when we least expected it.